Conflict and Fragility

Preventing Violence, War and State Collapse

THE FUTURE OF CONFLICT EARLY WARNING AND RESPONSE

D1666424

OECD

ORGANISATION FOR ECONOMIC CO-OPERATION AND DEVELOPMENT

The OECD is a unique forum where the governments of 30 democracies work together to address the economic, social and environmental challenges of globalisation. The OECD is also at the forefront of efforts to understand and to help governments respond to new developments and concerns, such as corporate governance, the information economy and the challenges of an ageing population. The Organisation provides a setting where governments can compare policy experiences, seek answers to common problems, identify good practice and work to co-ordinate domestic and international policies.

The OECD member countries are: Australia, Austria, Belgium, Canada, the Czech Republic, Denmark, Finland, France, Germany, Greece, Hungary, Iceland, Ireland, Italy, Japan, Korea, Luxembourg, Mexico, the Netherlands, New Zealand, Norway, Poland, Portugal, the Slovak Republic, Spain, Sweden, Switzerland, Turkey, the United Kingdom and the United States. The Commission of the European Communities takes part in the work of the OECD.

OECD Publishing disseminates widely the results of the Organisation's statistics gathering and research on economic, social and environmental issues, as well as the conventions, guidelines and standards agreed by its members.

This work is published on the responsibility of the Secretary-General of the OECD. The opinions expressed and arguments employed herein do not necessarily reflect the official views of the Organisation or of the governments of its member countries.

Also available in French under the title:
Conflits et fragilité
Prévenir la violence, la guerre et l'effondrement des États
L'AVENIR DES SYSTÈMES D'ALERTE PRÉCOCE ET DE RÉPONSE RAPIDE

Foreword

A considerable body of work has been carried out in recent years on the issue of early warning and response to violent conflict and fragile situations. Nevertheless, this publication suggests that it is questionable whether the international community would be capable of avoiding another genocide, as witnessed in Rwanda in 1994, were the situation to arise today.

It is against this background that *Preventing Violence, War and State Collapse: The Future of Conflict Early Warning and Response* identifies gaps in the early warning landscape, but also the opportunities that arise from current developments. In this way, the publication aims to support the efforts of OECD-DAC members and other organisations active in the field of conflict prevention and peacebuilding to better integrate early warning analysis and response into their programming.

The findings point out that many international organisations and bilateral development agencies have made progress in this area – they have integrated early warning mechanisms into their policies and strengthened institutional mandates for early responses. This is indeed an encouraging development. However, despite considerable intellectual and financial investments in this field over the past decade, the international community often fails to anticipate the consequences of clear warning signs of conflict and state fragility.

This publication argues that in the light of future conflict dynamics, international actors need to adapt their early warning systems and take advantage of ongoing technological evolutions and innovative Web 2.0 applications. The future role of OECD-DAC members in shaping further developments in this domain is therefore essential. Significantly, the publication highlights the role of regional and so-called "third generation" early warning systems and the critical need to work with local actors on the ground, both as early warners and as the first line of response. OECD-DAC members are also encouraged to assess the need for a more effective global and regional early warning architecture to overcome the problem of a fragmented approach.

Based on a comprehensive analysis with input from numerous surveys and interviews, this publication represents a milestone in bringing together the current state of play in the development of early warning and response systems and in recommending ways forward in this sensitive area. I am sure this work will be of direct value for policy makers in donor and partner countries, the academic community, regional and non-governmental organisations working on the issue of early warning and response.

Eckhard Deutscher

Chair

Development Assistance Committee

Acknowledgements

Contributions

The first acknowledgement due is to the many distinguished individuals and organisations that have developed the thinking and applied practice of conflict early warning over the past decades. This report draws very much on their work.

Special thanks go to Padmaja Barua, who provided invaluable research assistance. Stephan Massing and Rory Keane (OECD) provided critical guidance, support and feedback that are reflected throughout this document. The report also has benefited from the knowledge and perspectives of Kumar Rupesinghe (FCE), Marton Krasznai (UNECE), Celine Moyroud (UNDP), Samuel Doe (UNDP), Jane Alexander (DFID) and Oujin Paek (FCO). Prompt responses to questionnaires and queries were received from the German, French, Swiss, Canadian, Japanese, Spanish, New Zealand and United Kingdom governments. Special thanks also go to ECOWAS, IGAD, ECCAS, the World Bank, the European Commission, FEWER-Eurasia/Africa, swisspeace, ISS, FTI, FCE, Carleton University, The Fund for Peace and the George Mason University for completing questionnaires.

The author is deeply indebted to the peer reviewers who took time to read over and comment on early drafts of this report, including Guy Banim, Tobias Debiel, Anton Ivanov, Samuel Doe, Marton Krasznai, Dinidu Endaragalle, Patrick Meier (who provided valuable additions to both this report and the compendium), Tom Porteous and Kumar Rupesinghe. Editorial contributions were received from Tom Porteous and Patrick Meier, while valuable graphics/design support came from Manali Jagtap of Urban Guru Ltd. Also thanks to Helene Lavoix, whose initial mapping of early warning systems in 2007 was valuable.

A final thanks goes to Kumar Rupesinghe and Eugenia Piza-Lopez, who provided much guidance throughout the author's six years at FEWER. To Howard Adelman and Alejandro Bendaña, the author is indebted for shaping his academic and political thinking (respectively) on conflict early warning.

All errors and mistakes present in this report remain, nonetheless, the author's own responsibility.

About the author

David Nyheim is currently the Chief Executive of International Conflict and Security (INCAS) Consulting Ltd. (United Kingdom). He served for six years as the Director of the Forum for Early Warning and Early Response until 2003. During that period he worked extensively on early warning and preventive action in Africa and the Caucasus. He has also held several policy and research positions in the European Commission, Catholic University of Louvain, and London School of Hygiene and Tropical Medicine. As a consultant, he has worked for governments, United Nations agencies, and corporations in the North Caucasus, West Africa, South and Southeast Asia and the Pacific. He has published on a range of issues, including early warning, human rights, dialogue processes and conflict-sensitive development. David Nyheim is currently based out of Mumbai and London. E-mail: *david@incasconsulting.com*; website: *www.incasconsulting.com*.

Table of Contents

List of Abbreviations **10**

Executive Summary **13**

Introduction and background 13
Historical review of the early warning and response 13
Early warning tools and systems..14
Response tools and systems 15
Future directions for early warning and early response 17
Conclusions and recommendations..18

Introduction..**21**

Background 21
Key definitions..22
Critical questions..23
Structure of the report 24

Chapter 1. **A Short Contemporary History of Conflict Early Warning**.......**25**

From the first thinkers to policy integration..............................26
The initial debates 29
From tools to systems..32
First, second and third generation systems..............................34
Analytical conclusions 35

Chapter 2. **The Range of Early Warning Tools and Systems** **37**

The tools and methods 39
The operational early warning systems......................................48
Analytical conclusions 61

Chapter 3. **Is Early Early? A Review of Response Mechanisms and Instruments** **63**

Evaluating responses to violent conflict...66
The survey: early and rapid response mechanisms and instruments 69
The warning-response link 80
Analytical conclusions 83

Chapter 4. **Future Directions for Early Warning and Early Response** **85**

Future threats to international security...86
Advances in technology 89
Current trends in warning and response initiatives 90
Analytical conclusions 94

Chapter 5. **Conclusions and Recommendations**...**97**

What does it add up to?..98
Revisiting critical questions 99
Emerging questions and research needs...101
Recommendations for the OECD DAC 102

Bibliography...**105**

Annex. Compendium of Surveyed Early Warning Systems and Early Response Mechanisms/Instruments...........................**109**

Early warning systems 110
Early response mechanisms and instruments 127

Tables

Table 2.1. Quantitative models/ methods/systems – violent conflict
  and state fragility 39
Table 2.2. Qualitative models/methods – violent conflict and state fragility......46
Table 2.3. Governmental, inter-governmental, and non-governmental
  early warning systems 50
Table 3.1. Examples of operational and structural prevention..........................65
Table 3.2. Governmental, inter-governmental, and non-governmental
  early/rapid response mechanisms 71
Table 3.3. Personal, institutional, and political factors that affect response 81
Table 5.1. Strengths and weaknesses of quantitative and qualitative methods.100

Figures

Figure 2.1. Goldstein average domestic conflict and co-operation graph...........41
Figure 2.2. Failed States Index Score 2007 43
Figure 2.3. Early warning systems in the European region 52
Figure 2.4. Early warning systems in the African region....................................53
Figure 2.5. Early warning systems in the Asian region 56
Figure 3.1. The institutions, delivery mechanisms, and toolbox of
   responses to violent conflict 66
Figure 3.2. Organisational structure of the CEWARN mechanism 75
Figure 3.3. Unpacking the lack of political will..81
Figure 4.1. Risk map of conflict events in Afghanistan......................................90
Figure 4.2. Screenshot from the website of the Ushahidi initiative 91
Figure 4.3. Corporate conflict risk assessment tool 92

Boxes

Box 1.1. Integrated responses to conflict...32
Box 2.1. Basic theory behind Goldstein's conflict and co-operation model.......41
Box 2.2. Survey questions on early warning systems...49
Box 2.3. Case Study 1: The OSCE's early warning about the former
   Yugoslav Republic of Macedonia 58
Box 2.4. Good practice in operational conflict early warning systems..............59
Box 2.5. Lessons from the closure of FAST...60
Box 3.1. Survey questions on response delivery mechanisms and instruments..70
Box 3.2. Case Study 2: An early warning success story from CEWARN in
   Kenya/Uganda 76
Box 3.3. Case Study 3: An early response from the Foundation for
   Co-Existence in the Eastern Province...78
Box 4.1. Climate-related threats to international security – High
   Representative and European Commission Report to the
   European Council, March 2008..87
Box 4.2. Main findings of OECD DAC thematic meetings on
   whole-of-government approaches 93

List of Abbreviations

ACP	African, Caribbean and Pacific
APFO	Africa Peace Forum
AU	African Union
BMZ	Federal Ministry for Economic Cooperation and Development (Germany)
CDA Inc.	Collaborative Learning Projects
CEWARN	Conflict Early Warning and Response Mechanism
CEWERU	Conflict Early Warning and Early Response Unit
CEWS	Continental Early Warning System
CFSP	Common Foreign and Security Policy
CIDA	Canadian International Development Agency
CIFP	Country Indicators for Foreign Policy
CPDC	Conflict Peace and Development Co-operation Network
CPP	Conflict Prevention Pool
CPR Network	Conflict Prevention and Reconstruction Network
DFAIT	Department for Foreign Affairs and International Trade (Canada)
DFID	Department for International Development (UK)
EAWARN	Network for Ethnological Monitoring and Early Warning
ECCAS	Economic Community of Central African States
ECOWARN	ECOWAS Early Warning and Response Network
ECOWAS	Economic Community Of West African States
EDF	European Development Fund
EISAS	Information and Strategic Analysis Secretariat
EU	European Union
EUSITCEN	European Union Situation Centre
FAST	Early Recognition and Analysis of Tensions
FCE	Foundation for Coexistence
FEWER	Forum on Early Warning and Early Response
FEWER-Africa	Forum on Early Warning and Early Response-Africa
FEWER-Eurasia	Forum on Early Warning and Early Response-Eurasia
FSG	Fragile States Group
GCPP	Global Conflict Prevention Pool
GEDS	Global Events Data System

GIGAS	German Institute for Global Area Studies
GTZ	*Deutsche Gesellschaft für Technische Zusammenarbeit*
HMT	Her Majesty's Treasury
ICG	International Crisis Group
IGAD	Inter-Governmental Authority on Development
IGO	Inter-governmental organisation
ISS	Institute for Security Studies
KEDS	Kansas Events Data System
LICUS	Low Income Countries Under Stress
LTTE	Liberation Tigers of Tamil Eelam
MARAC	Mécanisme d'alerte rapide de l'Afrique centrale
MOD	Ministry of Defence
NATO	North Atlantic Treaty Organisation
NGO	Non-governmental organisation
OAU	Organisation of African Unity (now AU)
OECD	Organisation for Economic Co-operation and Development
OSCE	Organization for Security and Co-operation in Europe
PANDA	Protocol for the Analysis of Nonviolent Direct Action
PCIA	Peace and Conflict Impact Assessment
PITF	Political Instability Task Force
PPEWU	Policy Planning and Early Warning Unit (EU)
SADC	Southern African Development Community
SAP	*Système d'Alerte Précoce* (France)
START	Stabilisation and Reconstruction Task Force (Canada)
UN	United Nations
UNDHA	United Nations Department for Humanitarian Affairs (now UNOCHA)
UNDP	United Nations Development Programme
UNDPA	United Nations Department for Political Affairs
UNHCR	United Nations High Commissioner for Refugees
UNIFEM	United Nations Fund for Women
UNOCHA	United Nations Office for the Coordination of Humanitarian Affairs
USAID	United States Agency for International Development
VRA	Virtual Research Associates
WANEP	West Africa Network for Peacebuilding
WARN	West Africa Early Warning and Response Network

Executive Summary

Introduction and background

The aim of this report is to support the efforts of OECD DAC members and others to better integrate conflict early warning analysis and response into their programming. The report is based on a review of the literature on early warning and response and inputs from surveyed agencies. It seeks to assess the value and role of early warning for the prevention of violent conflict and peacebuilding; identify the most effective early warning and response systems; evaluate the strengths and weaknesses of different systems; pinpoint the obstacles to early response; and make some tentative judgements on what the role of OECD DAC could be in influencing future developments in this field.

Historical review of the early warning and response

Conflict early warning was conceived as a means of protecting and preserving life. The field has evolved significantly since its initial conceptualisation, and early warning has been integrated into the policies of many organisations. Today it cannot be said, however, that the international community is in a position to prevent another Rwandan genocide. Conflict early warning faces challenges similar to those it faced 15 years ago – and there are new challenges on the horizon.

From initial conceptualisation in the 1970s and 1980s, conflict early warning only really emerged on the international policy agenda after the end of the Cold War, when the conflict environment and the international conflict management framework evolved rapidly in response to the new geo-strategic reality. The failure to respond to the Rwandan genocide in 1994 and the experiences of the Balkans conflicts were major spurs to the development of better conflict early warning and response; they led to several major policy initiatives in governmental, inter-governmental and non-governmental sectors.

From the start, conflict early warning was envisaged as distinct from intelligence-based analysis that focused on protection of state interests. It sought multi-stakeholder solutions, was gender-sensitive, used open source information and aimed at protecting human lives and creating sustainable peace based on locally owned solutions. However, this approach has been overshadowed by the new Northern perception of international threats that emerged after the terrorist attacks of 11 September 2001 and consequent counterterrorism and counter-proliferation measures taken by the United States and its allies. Those attacks also acted as a spur to growing interest in and analysis of weak, fragile and failed states.

In spite of the increased resources going into early warning, key shortcomings of governmental and multilateral interventions in violent conflict remain. These include faulty analysis, late, uncoordinated and contradictory engagement, and poor decision making.

Conflict early warning as a field of conflict prevention is today undergoing significant scrutiny. There have been inaccurate predictions, failure to foresee important events, and inadequate linking of operational responses to warnings. From a donor perspective, the visible impacts of early warning are often seen as meagre. Indeed, at times early warning analyses can provide donor officials with political headaches, by being alarmist or offensive to other governments, or by advocating responses that are not feasible. However, proponents of conflict early warning insist that it contributes to the evidence base of conflict prevention decision making.

Early warning tools and systems

The focus of this report is on tools/systems that deal with violent conflict and state fragility.

The evolution of the conflict early warning field has been driven by the advances made in quantitative and qualitative analytical tools. As the capabilities and value of the tools grew, they were integrated into the different early warning systems operated by governments, inter-governmental organisations, and NGOs.

Such tools have enjoyed significant advances. Quantitative methods have strong predictive capabilities, particularly in relation to political crisis and instability. State fragility indices provide easily graspable "watch lists" and help agencies working on these issues to set priorities. Qualitative methods provide rich contextual analysis, as well as ways to plan programmatic responses and assess the impact of these responses on violent conflicts. The more recent qualitative methods for state fragility analysis provide useful planning frameworks for programmatic responses.

Qualitative tools satisfy important analytical requirements among development agencies, particularly in terms of informing programming. Nonetheless, numerous weaknesses persist. Analytical tools fundamentally oversimplify complex and fluid violent conflicts and situations of state fragility. They provide simple snapshots that are quickly outdated, and the quality of analysis suffers from data deficits that characterise many of the countries covered by such studies.

Two conclusions can be drawn when it comes to quantitative and qualitative tools. First, there is no "best methodology" or "best set of indicators": there is basic good practice in analysis. Many methods are based on this good practice and are designed to address the needs of specific institutions. Second, the best way to use these methods is to combine quantitative and qualitative tools. This ensures the necessary triangulation required for creating a robust evidence base for decision making.

Early warning systems now exist within governments, multilateral agencies and NGOs. They play different roles – ranging from sounding alerts and catalysing response, to bolstering the evidence base of decision making, to serving as response mechanisms themselves. There is consensus on what constitutes a "good" early warning system, and this good practice has been put into operation in several initiatives. Early warning systems provide: a crisis prediction capacity that enables proactive decision making; a stronger basis for evidence-based decision making on countries affected by crisis; improved programming through systematic country reviews and expert analysis; a priority-setting contribution through watch-list type products; a starting point for developing a shared problem definition for crisis-affected countries that sets the stage for more coherent responses; and an ideas pool for responses and sometimes the forum to meet fellow responders and plan joint response strategies. However, with a few exceptions, early warning systems suffer from under-investment. The more natural clients for early warning systems are political decision-making entities.

Still, the often poor/shallow quality of analyses, unrealistic recommendations, and biased or ungrounded opinions present in many early warning products means that "poor early warning" remains an important cause of non-response to violent conflict. *What is poor early warning?*

Response tools and systems

Advances over the last 15 years or so in early and rapid response have been made in the range of institutions, mechanisms, instruments and processes available to manage violent conflict – and in national, regional and international willingness to use force in situations of violent conflict. At national, regional and international levels, capabilities to respond to situations of violent conflict and state fragility have evolved significantly. Institutional mandates for response have been strengthened, funding has increased, there is a greater range of operational tools, and mechanisms have been refined on the basis of applied experience. However, the multiplicity of actors and responses means that the problems of late, incoherent, fragmented, and confused response are perhaps greater today than was true at the time of the Rwandan genocide.

Numerous challenges are identified in the literature and in the survey of practitioners carried out by this study. First, the role of analytical evidence in determining response (as opposed to political expediency, budgetary considerations, etc.) remains limited. Second, *ad hocism* and limited strategic thinking is prevalent. Many actors do not define or share a clear strategy for supporting peace in violent conflict situations. The absence of such strategic frameworks leads to incoherence and uncoordinated responses. Third, sustainability concerns remain unaddressed. Whether related to macro-level strategies for stabilisation or sector-specific approaches, responses are rarely designed to outlast themselves. Fourth, stove piped responses, based on narrow institutional interests have not been overcome. Deep divisions between security and development agencies and a propensity for "blueprints" in responses to different countries with problems perceived as similar remain cause for concern.

From evaluations of responses to violent conflict, several "good practice" principles have been drawn by scholars, including: *(a)* understand the problem, base analysis on evidence from the ground; *(b)* ensure that responses are diverse, flexible, and sustainable; *(c)* invest time in planning and strategy; *(d)* be conflict-sensitive; *(e)* don't push technical solutions onto political problems; *(f)* balance speed, ownership and co-ordination. This review identifies a number of important gains from the development of governmental, inter-governmental and non-governmental response mechanisms/instruments, including: more rapid, coherent, and informed responses within institutions to situations of violent conflict and state fragility; the potential for reducing costs associated to expensive "late" responses to violent conflict and state fragility; the promotion of more consensus-based decision making within both the bureaucracies and political leadership in crisis situations; and their role as a resource to help avoid the derailment of developmental investments by crises and conflict.

However, more mechanisms/instruments have not translated into better responses. The link between warning and response remains weak. This is due to the poor quality of early warning and immature mechanisms/instruments and response measures, along with a range of personal, institutional, and political shortcomings that affect decision making. If the problem was formerly that "early warning is not wired to the bulb", today it may be that there are too many "bulbs" competing with each other or not working when they should.

Future directions for early warning and early response

Early warning and early response will be faced with an evolution of threats over the next decade. These threats will come from the combined impacts on conflict and instability of climate change, fallout from the wars in Afghanistan and Iraq, fallout from the war on terror, and the increasing criminalisation of conflict, among other factors. There is little indication of forward thinking among early warners on these critical issues. However, the future relevance of the field depends largely on work undertaken now to be able to understand and provide useful analysis on these new emerging threats.

Technological advancements have played an important role in improving the efficiency and effectiveness of early warning systems. Most inter-governmental and non-governmental systems, however, have not gone beyond the use of email and websites for dissemination, and communication technology for data collection. Governmental and some inter-governmental systems do benefit from access to and resources for satellites and GIS in their analysis and reporting. However, access to technology remains very unequal among systems and the field of conflict early warning lags far behind in the use of innovative technologies and Web 2.0 applications.

There are several important trends in the early warning community that should be noted. First, with the closure of FEWER and FAST, there is now less diversity in early warning analysis at a global level. Exclusive reliance on few sources, no matter how good they are, is not smart decision-making practice, particularly in complex issues such as violent conflict and state fragility. Second, development agencies working on structural prevention see less value in early warning than before. Agencies involved in operational prevention remain interested, but current early warning systems need to consider how to shift their networking efforts to these actors if they have not done so already. Third, with increased corporate use of early warning and risk assessment tools, there are new partners to bring into the early warning fold.

In terms of early response trends, the following conclusions can be drawn. First, along with work to ensure greater governmental and inter-governmental coherence, there is a need to empower officials working on conflict and state fragility (through capacity building, etc.) to do their work well. Second, an increase in response capabilities and experience needs to be bolstered by initiatives to document and share good practice. Not doing so will constitute a missed opportunity. Third, micro-level responses to violent conflict by "third generation early warning systems" are an exciting development in the field that should be encouraged further. These kinds of responses save lives.

Conclusions and recommendations

Considering the balance between future security threats and trends in technology, early warning, and early response, this report concludes that the early warning and response field is unprepared for the challenges that it is likely to face over the next decades.

The report concludes with a number of recommendations, including:

1. Assist in the consolidation of good (quantitative and qualitative) methodological and applied reporting practice for conflict analysis and state fragility analysis.

The consolidation of good methodological practice needs to focus on both methods and their application (see Chapters 1 and 2). It needs to include the following:

- The organisation of a conflict and state fragility analysis workshop that brings together method developers to discuss and document good practice. Topics covered should include how different (quantitative and qualitative) methods can best be combined to yield a more robust evidence base for decision making.

- Increased funding of efforts to develop more applied qualitative state fragility assessments – particularly as these relate to institutional planning cycles and impact assessments of efforts to reduce state fragility. This is a very new area and the DAC may have a comparative advantage here.

- Explore further (through applied research) how state fragility indices or assessments can be used to better inform resource allocations and what their limitations are for that purpose. This would entail expanding the DAC work on monitoring resource allocation by monitoring how resources are allocated in relation to state fragility – and the strengths/weaknesses of basing resource allocations on "watch list"-type assessments.

- Prepare a short DAC "recommended reporting standards" document for conflict analysis, early warning and state fragility reports, and disseminate these broadly as part of ensuring improved reporting on violent conflict and state fragility. Such reporting standards will provide important benchmarks for early warners to attain, and will help improve how analytical methods are applied.

- Concretely outline the critical importance of adopting innovative information communication technologies for data collection, communication, visualisation and analysis.

2. Consider how early warning systems can promote improved understanding of armed violence dynamics (see Chapter 4).

- An indicator list based on case studies is required to help identify what factors early warners need to analyse when operating systems in areas affected by armed violence. Such (non-prescriptive) indicators should include those related to, *inter alia,* the political economy of violence and supply and demand of weapons.

- More sophisticated methods for stakeholder analysis are required to capture group motivations (beyond grievance) and relationships, especially given the importance of group and leadership culture and psychology in violent conflict situations.

3. Consider the need for a bolstered global early warning and response architecture (see Chapters 2, 3 and 4).

- Consider how a shared, diversified and more robust evidence base for decision making on violent conflict and state fragility can be created – particularly in view of the reduced number of global sources of analysis and the need to align current early warning systems (and funding pools) with political (as opposed to developmental) decision makers. Explore the establishment of a new global network for early warning and response (involving regional organisations, governments, and non-governmental agencies) to address this deficit.

- Endorse efforts to build internal capacity and functional external relations among staff dealing with conflict-affected countries and situations of state fragility. Capacity building needs to involve skills development, and internal reviews of existing institutional processes that enable (or disable) officials from pursuing appropriate and rapid responses.

- Promote the practice of regular assessments of "whole-of-system" responses to violent conflict and state fragility situations (along the lines of the Rwanda Joint Evaluation) to build the knowledge base from the applied "do's and don'ts". Ensure that the reviews both tackle the institutional mechanism/instrument and measure dimensions of responses.

- Call for the standard use of multi-stakeholder platforms for joint problem definition and planning of responses to situations of violent conflict and state fragility. Ensure that such platforms include both state and civil society groups, along with regional and international organisations.

- Consider how well placed (or not) current regional and international early warning and response capabilities are to assess and respond to global current and future security threats. This could involve calling for a high-level meeting to review the current global conflict early warning and response architecture.

4. Increase support for regional early warning systems, and third generation systems that address micro-level violence.

There is a need to invest more effectively in conflict early warning systems. Such investment should be focused on the early warning efforts of regional organisations and those of non-governmental organisations that fall into the category of third generation systems (see Chapters 1 and 2).

- Investments in the early warning efforts of regional organisations need to focus on bolstering: *(a)* the quality of reporting; *(b)* the warning-response link; and *(c)* sensitivity among senior policy making of the value of evidence-based decision making in situations of violent conflict and state fragility.

- Investments in third generation systems need to be focused on strengthening the institutional capacities of operating organisations. This needs to include core funding for permanent staff, funding for capacity building, access to technology, and other network running costs.

- All regional and third generation systems need to be encouraged to consider how their efforts could be adjusted to enable analysis and response to future security threats. Bringing these groups together onto a broad global platform can also facilitate the exchange of lessons learned and cross-fertilisation of good practice.

Introduction

Background

This report has been commissioned by the OECD DAC Conflict Peace and Development Co-operation Network (CPDC) and the Fragile States Group (FSG) as part of the joint workstream on early warning, preventive action, and collective response.

The aim of the report (and indeed of the workstream itself) is to support the efforts of OECD DAC members and other governmental, multilateral and NGO partners to better integrate early warning analysis and response into their programming. The research leading to this report was carried out over five months (December 2007 – April 2008) and involved:

- A web-based review of articles, papers and books on early warning and early response, including good practice, tools and systems.

- A questionnaire survey on early warning and early response to CPDC and FSG members and other partners.

- A questionnaire survey on key methodologies sent to selected agencies involved in the development of such methodologies.

- Meetings and telephone discussions with key respondents on issues that required further investigation.

- Analysis of findings and drafting of the report, including a peer review exercise with key experts in the field.

- Incorporation of feedback from the peer review and client into a final draft report that was circulated to CPDC and FSG members for comment.

In September 2008, the OECD DAC commissioned Patrick Meier (Harvard Humanitarian Initiative) to review the report and compendium.

The reader of this report should keep the following caveats in mind:

- Because of the needs of the target audience of the report, the emphasis is placed on the operational application of early warning tools and systems rather than on theoretical and academic issues.

- The report does not review all existing early warning tools and systems. It is based on responses from surveyed agencies and a review of the tools/systems used by policy makers in selected institutions.

- The report does not review all existing early response mechanisms and instruments. Rather, it is focused on a selection of funding and expertise mechanisms/instruments used by OECD DAC members and multilateral agencies, along with a sample of NGO-led response mechanisms.

- The definitions used for "early warning", "early response" necessarily restrict what is covered in this report. However, discretion has been used to expand coverage when deemed appropriate.

- The "open source" focus of the report means that intelligence-based systems (found particularly in government agencies) are not reviewed in this report.

Key definitions

The scope of the report rests heavily on the definitions used. Among these are the following:

- *Early warning* is a process that *(a)* alerts decision makers to the potential outbreak, escalation and resurgence of violent conflict; and *(b)* promotes an understanding among decision makers of the nature and impacts of violent conflict (adapted from FEWER in Schmid, 1998).

- *Early warning systems* involve regular and organised collection and analysis of information on violent conflict situations. They deliver a set of early warning products (based on qualitative and/or quantitative conflict analysis methods) that are linked to response instruments/mechanisms (adapted from FEWER in Schmid, 1998).

- *Early and rapid response* refers to any initiative that occurs as soon as the threat of potential violent conflict is identified and that aims to manage, resolve, or prevent that violent conflict.

- *Early/rapid response systems* are one or several preventive instruments and mechanisms (political, economic/financial, social, security) informed by an early warning that are deployed to manage, resolve, or prevent the outbreak, escalation, and resurgence of violent conflict.

- *Fragile, weak and failing states* are defined here as "countries that lack the essential capacity and/or will to fulfil four sets of critical government responsibilities: fostering an environment conducive to sustainable and equitable economic growth; establishing and maintaining legitimate, transparent, and accountable political institutions; securing their populations from violent conflict and controlling their territory; and meeting the basic human needs of their population" (Rice and Stewart, 2008).

Critical questions

This report seeks to shed light on the following critical questions:

- What is the value of early warning for the prevention of violent conflict and peacebuilding? What role does early warning play in prevention?

- What are the most effective early warning systems? Why are they effective and what impacts do they have?

- What are the comparative strengths and weaknesses of different methodologies – *e.g.* quantitative *vs.* qualitative analysis, and conflict analysis *vs.* assessment of state fragility?

- What does it take to prevent violent conflict? What do we currently know is good practice and what works?

- What early/rapid response mechanisms/instruments are available?

- What influences and blocks early response? What are the personal, institutional and political factors at play?

- Where should the early warning/response field go from here? What role should the OECD DAC play?

These questions are answered in different chapters of the report and revisited in the concluding chapter.

Structure of the report

The report seeks to explore these questions in five chapters:

- *A Short Contemporary History of Conflict Early Warning* (Chapter 1). This chapter covers the integration of early warning into the mandates of different agencies, the evolution of early warning tools into systems, the paradigms underpinning warning and response, and the transition from first to second to third generation early warning and response systems.

- *The Range of Early Warning Tools and Systems* (Chapter 2). This chapter includes a review of governmental, inter-governmental and non-governmental quantitative and qualitative tools and methods of analysis, and a discussion of current operational early warning systems.

- *Is Early Early? A Review of Response Mechanisms and Instruments* (Chapter 3). This chapter briefly reviews challenges and lessons for responses to violent conflict; provides an analysis of a cross-section of response mechanisms and instruments; and discusses the warning-response link.

- *Future Directions for Early Warning and Early Response* (Chapter 4). This chapter discusses some of the possible future trends in early warning and early response and the potential impact of emerging security threats and technological advances.

- *Conclusions and Recommendations* (Chapter 5). This chapter reviews critical questions and the answers given in the report and concludes with recommendations for the OECD DAC.

A Compendium of Surveyed Early Warning Systems and Early Response Mechanisms/Instruments, with profiles, is attached as annex to this report.

Chapter 1

A Short Contemporary History of Conflict Early Warning

Charting a short history of the conflict early warning field is not easy. The field draws heavily on work in many sectors (early warning for natural disasters for example), and has benefited from thinking, research and advocacy by numerous individuals and organisations. This chapter seeks to explain initial thinking behind conflict early warning and looks at its emergence on the international policy agenda. It outlines the evolution of operational early warning systems after the end of the Cold War and particularly after the Rwandan genocide in 1994. It reviews the initial debates among implementing organisations and discusses the evolution of different tools and methods (e.g. conflict assessment and analysis of state fragility) and of individual operational early warning systems. The chapter concludes with a review of the main points of criticism and challenges with which proponents of conflict early warning need to engage

Conflict early warning was conceived as a means of protecting and preserving life. The field has evolved significantly since its initial conceptualisation, with important contributions from many individuals and organisations over the years. Early warning has been integrated into the policies of many governmental, inter-governmental and non-governmental organisations and agencies. Both the concept of early warning and individual systems have been subject to numerous reviews and debates. Many different tools and methodologies have been developed. We have witnessed the rise (and fall) of a number of different early warning systems. However, can we say today that we are in a position to prevent another Rwandan genocide? We cannot. Conflict early warning faces response challenges similar to those it faced 15 years ago. And there are new challenges on the horizon. Our ability to protect and preserve life in the face of war remains weak as Darfur, DR Congo and Iraq show all too clearly

From the first thinkers to policy integration

Conceptualisation of early warning as applied to violent conflict gained momentum as early as the 1970s and early 80s. As explained by Rupesinghe (1989), thinkers such as J. David Singer (Singer and Wallace, 1979) applied forecasting to war and Israel Charney (Charney and Charney, 1982) explored the application of early warning to genocide prevention. Specific international proposals for an early warning system were made by the Special Rapporteur, Prince Sadruddin Aga Khan in his report on Massive Exodus and Human Rights delivered to the UN Economic and Social Council Commission on Human Rights on 31 December 1981 (Rupesinghe, 1989). In 1987, the UN set up the Office for the Research and Collection of Information (ORCI) to develop an early warning system dedicated to monitoring and analysing global trends.

However, the initial drivers of early warning at an international level were humanitarian agencies (UNHCR, UNDHA and others) spurred by the need for accurate and timely predictions of refugee flows to enable effective contingency planning. Establishment of the first conflict prevention NGOs, such as International Alert in 1985, and their advocacy for early warning also pushed thinking forward internationally.

The end of the Cold War had a positive impact on the international framework for conflict prevention, enabling among other things sustained co-operation on conflict management, including conflict prevention in the UN Security Council. At the same time, the end of the Cold War had both negative and positive impacts on the evolution of conflict environments in various parts of the world. In some areas it contributed to an easing of tension and the end of long-running conflicts. In others it triggered new conflicts and transformed old ones into new kinds of armed struggles. International policy makers were forced to focus on new intra-state conflicts in the Horn of Africa, West Africa, the Balkans and elsewhere.

These developments were behind the June 1992 report to the Security Council of the United Nations Secretary-General Boutros Boutros-Ghali, "An Agenda for Peace, Preventive Diplomacy, Peacemaking, and Peace-Keeping". In it, he laid out aims for UN engagement, the first being "to seek to identify at the earliest possible stage situations that could produce conflict and to try through diplomacy to remove the sources of danger before violence erupts." "Preventive steps", the report also said, "must be based upon timely and accurate knowledge of the facts. Beyond this, an understanding of developments and global trends, based on sound analysis, is required. And the willingness to take appropriate preventive action is essential" (United Nations, 1992). At a regional level, policy integration moved a step closer to implementation in June 1992 with the formal initiation by the OAU of the Mechanism for Conflict Prevention, Management and Resolution, a unit for conflict early warning in Africa (Cilliers, 2005), though it took some time for this to develop into anything very effective.

The failure to prevent the Rwandan genocide in 1994 underlined the weaknesses of regional and international mechanisms for early warning of and response to mass violence. The multi-government evaluation of the international response to the Rwandan genocide concluded that "pieces of information were available that, if put together and analyzed, would have permitted policy-makers to draw the conclusion that both political assassinations and genocide might occur" (Steering Committee of the Joint Evaluation of Emergency Assistance to Rwanda, 1996). These conclusions and the critical questions raised in the report – why were the signals that were sent ignored, and why were they not translated into effective conflict management? – spurred several international policy initiatives.

- The *OECD DAC Guidelines on Conflict, Peace, and Development Co-operation* (1997) specified the importance of conflict early warning in catalysing early response. The *Guidelines* highlighted the need to support networks with early warning, monitoring and analytical capabilities.

- The Final Report of the Carnegie Commission on Preventing Deadly Conflict (1997) stressed the need for early warning, stating that "the circumstances that give rise to violent conflict can usually be foreseen. This was certainly true of violence in Bosnia in 1992 and in Rwanda in 1994." The Final Report also underlined the need for local solutions to violent conflict and the need for early international responses to support these.

- The *Report of the Panel on United Nations Peace Operations* (United Nations, 2000), commonly known as the "Brahimi Report", placed early warning within the broader framework of UN peacekeeping, stating that "without such a capacity, the Secretariat will remain a reactive institution, unable to get ahead of daily events…". The proposed Information and Strategic Analysis Secretariat (EISAS) was to consolidate the existing DPKO Situation Centre with other policy planning offices but it was never implemented due to member state sensitivities.

- The "Brahimi Report" was followed by several policy papers issued by donor governments. The United Kingdom's 2000 White Paper on International Development, for example, called for the implementation of the "Brahimi Report" within 12 months, and spelled out the UK government's strategy for greater cohesion in its own engagement on conflict prevention. This included the establishment of the Global and Africa Conflict Prevention Pools (United Kingdom Government, 2000).

- At a sub-regional level, IGAD heads of state issued the *Khartoum Declaration* in 2000, stating, "We endorse the establishment of a mechanism in the IGAD sub-region for prevention, management, and resolution of intra-state and inter-state conflicts, and direct the Executive Secretary to prepare a draft protocol on the establishment of the Conflict Early Warning and Response Mechanism (CEWARN) for consideration by the assembly at its next meeting" (IGAD, 2000).

- The UN Secretary General's *Prevention of Armed Conflict: Report of the Secretary General* in 2001 stressed the need for the Secretariat's Department of Political Affairs to strengthen its capacity to carry out conflict analysis in countries prone to or affected by conflict. It stated that the "timely application of preventive diplomacy has been recognised by the General Assembly as the most desirable and efficient means for easing tensions before they result in conflict" (United Nations, 2001).

- The European Commission's *Communication from the Commission on Conflict Prevention* in 2001 included statements on the link between early warning and various Commission and Council instruments, stating that "A capacity for troubleshooting depends crucially on the existence of a proper EU early warning mechanism, not only to alert EU decision making and operational centres to an imminent crisis but also to study its causes and possible consequences and identify the most appropriate response" (European Commission, 2001).

The initial debates

The period immediately after the genocide in Rwanda saw the establishment of several early warning initiatives in the academic and NGO community, including the establishment of the Forum on Early Warning and Early Response (FEWER),[1] the West Africa Network for Peacebuilding (WANEP),[2] the Network for Ethnological Monitoring and Early Warning (EAWARN), and the Early Recognition and Analysis of Tensions (FAST), an initiative of swisspeace. The initial debates among operational groups involved in early warning of conflict were focused on the purpose of early warning, the differences between conflict early warning and traditional intelligence work, gender considerations, the constituency and ownership of early warning systems, paradigms, and the link between warning and response.

The purpose of early warning

There were two strands to the debates on the purpose of early warning among operational agencies. On the one hand, some argued that early warning should serve as a tool to predict the outbreak, escalation, or resurgence of violent conflict. According to this school of thought, early warning analysis as an exercise should also be kept separately from advocacy efforts on response. Such a separation was seen as necessary to ensure that early warning analysis did not lose rigour because of a need to promote one response option or another. In other words, it was deemed important that early warning analysis not be politicised.

The other argument countered this by saying that simply predicting or providing analysis on whether violence will erupt (and lives will be lost) in a given area was not in the interests of the populations living there. Rather, early warning should be linked to strong response mechanisms and advocacy efforts at national, regional, and international levels *to save lives*. This was much in the spirit of the recommendations of the Rwanda Joint Evaluation.

Early warning versus traditional intelligence

The risks of conflating early warning with traditional intelligence work were a key concern as systems became operational. What distinguished the work of an early warning system from that of an intelligence agency? Maintaining a well-defined and well-publicised distinction became critical for any early warning system present in areas affected by violent conflict. Perceptions that intelligence gathering and early warning were one and the same could also greatly undermine the security of personnel and their ability to operate.

The distinction was derived from the roots of conflict early warning. As Adelman (2006) explains, early warning systems "followed the pattern of climate and humanitarian-based early warning systems in adopting a global perspective and not looking at potential or actual violence from the perspective of the threat to one's own state. Further, early warning relied primarily upon open sources in adopting a non state-centred approach to conflict management." The reliance on open source information is important. The pursuit of multi-stakeholder solutions to conflict means that there is a dependence on transparent methods of collecting and sharing of information (Cilliers, 2005). The key issue that settled the debate on what makes early warning distinct from intelligence is the former's exclusive use of open source information, analysis that is shared across groups, systems that do not serve state interests but the interests of peace, and the multiple stakeholders involved in the process of early warning and response.

Gender sensitivity

Initial work on operational early warning benefited significantly from concurrent initiatives on gender and peacebuilding. The work in those areas carried out by organisations such as UNIFEM, International Alert and swisspeace highlighted the need for gender sensitivity in early warning. In particular, a system that does *not* adopt a gender-sensitive approach:

- May overlook indicators of conflict and peace that are rooted in negative gender relations.

- May formulate response recommendations that inadvertently are harmful to women or detrimental to harmonious gender relations.

- May overlook important female actors and stakeholders, along with capacities for peace and violence.

For an excellent review of these issues, see Schmeidl and Piza-Lopez, 2002.

Constituency and ownership

In providing recommendations for response, those working in early warning were quickly faced with the question of "whose peace" they promoted. What interests, some would ask, are promoted in recommendations of organisations like International Crisis Group (ICG) or FEWER? What constituency is represented?

The question of constituency was and remains closely related to the question of legitimacy, particularly for southern civil society groups. Issuing recommendations for response as an external expert group is very different from doing so as a civil society network from a conflict-affected region. The question of constituency is also closely related to the question of ownership. Locally defined solutions, some groups argue, are more sustainable, as local ownership is a prerequisite for sustainability.

The constituency debate is in turn related to whether early warning systems perpetuate an interventionist paradigm, an issue discussed below.

Paradigm challenges

The paradigm within which conflict early warning was initially conceived was challenged in several ways by civil society groups working on conflict management in conflict-affected regions. They pointed out that:

- Most early warning systems would extract information from conflict areas and use this to inform interventions by northern governments (Barrs, 2006).

- International responses generally were plagued by inconsistency, lack of co-ordination and political bias, aside from generally being reactive and "late".

- A state-centric focus in conflict management does not reflect an understanding of the role played by civil society organisations in situations where the state has failed.

- An external, interventionist, and state-centric approach in early warning fuels disjointed and top-down responses in situations that require integrated and multilevel action.

These arguments were reinforced by academic research on conflict management (see for example Smith, 2003) and also gained traction among some donor agencies (*e.g.* USAID and agencies in Germany, Finland, Sweden, Denmark, and later Norway and the United Kingdom). Funding was given to regionally based early warning systems led by local organisations such as WANEP's WARN, or regional bodies such as IGAD's CEWARN.

The warning-response link

The 1996 Rwanda Joint Evaluation provided important insights into the shortcomings of governmental and multilateral interventions in violent conflict. It highlighted late, uncoordinated and contradictory engagement, as well as a range of political, institutional and individual failings and errors on the part of decision makers. All these shortcomings remain present in contemporary international responses to violent conflicts.

With the call by the "Brahimi Report" for greater coherence in conflict management, efforts to promote more streamlined and integrated responses to conflict picked up momentum. In the donor community, the OECD/DAC forum pushed forward good practice in policy and programming. Some donor governments launched important joined-up government approaches, including the UK government's Global and Africa Conflict Prevention Pools (CPP). In the NGO sector, there were several other initiatives (see Box 1.1). However, the link between warning and response has remained weak, as evidenced in the Kenya and Chad crises in 2007 and 2008. A more detailed discussion of the link between warning and response follows in Chapter 3.

Box 1.1. **Integrated responses to conflict**

FEWER, WANEP, EastWest Institute, and the OSCE Conflict Prevention Centre launched in 2001 a roundtable process that brought state and non-state (local, national and international) decision makers together to formulate joint response strategies to early warnings. The initiative was piloted in Georgia (Javakheti) and Guinea-Conakry, and later replicated in other early warning systems (EAWARN, WARN, FAST, etc.).

From tools to systems

A critical question in conflict early warning, especially in the early days, was what methodologies are best suited to predict violent conflict and/or better understand its nature. Much research was done in the 1990s by American academics in particular, to develop (mostly quantitative) methods of analysis. Initiatives such as Minorities at Risk, Global Events Data Systems (GEDS), Protocol for the Analysis of Nonviolent Direct Action

(PANDA), and others developed a strong empirical base for theories of violent conflict and advanced significantly on the coding (automated and manual) of information.[3] Work also started towards the end of the 1990s on several qualitative conflict analysis methods (*e.g.* the early methodology by The Fund for Peace, FEWER, USAID, World Bank, and DFID) that linked conflict analysis with stakeholder analysis and later, peace analysis (*e.g.* capacities for peace, peace indicators, conflict carrying capacities).

The fragile states agenda emerged later from a convergence of thinking on links between: human security and peacebuilding; state effectiveness and development performance; and underdevelopment and insecurity. The 2001 terrorist attacks on the United States and the view that fragile states are likely to generate (or fail to manage effectively) global security threats catalysed this already emerging international agenda (Cammack *et al.*, 2006).

Several initiatives have been launched to develop indices and lists of fragile states. Intended to guide aid prioritisation, these include DFID's proxy list of fragile states, George Mason University's State Fragility Index, The Fund for Peace "Failed States Index", the "Peace and Conflict Instability Ledger" of the University of Maryland, Carleton University's Country Indicators for Foreign Policy Project, the Brookings Institution's Index of State Weakness, and the work of the Center for Global Development.

Other groups have sought to develop guidelines for planning and programming in fragile states. Planning and programming methodologies have been prepared by the Canadian International Development Agency (CIDA), DFID, the Netherlands Ministry for Foreign Affairs, and the UK government's Cabinet Office. What has remained a challenge is the absence of a comprehensive and measurable definition of state fragility. The field is too young to define what constitutes good practice in these indices and methods. A more detail discussion of the fragile states agenda follows in Chapter 2.

Work on conflict early warning systems took place in parallel with the development of new methods of conflict analysis. Some government agencies, such as the German Ministry for Development Co-operation (BMZ), developed indicator checklists (also used by the European Commission) that initially were to be completed by embassy staff (now they are completed by external experts and reviewed internally) in countries seen as being at risk of violent conflict. Among the multilaterals, the OSCE High Commissioner for National Minorities set up several local early warning networks (*e.g.* Macedonia) to provide it with relevant information and analysis (see Case Study 1 in Chapter 2).

In addition, there was work on the development of advanced systems in the non-governmental sector. Agencies such as EAWARN, WANEP, the Africa Peace Forum (APFO) and later swisspeace/FAST, set up networks of local monitors and linked these to other sources of information, trained analysts in different methods of analysis, established formats and protocols for reporting and communication, and found targeted and broad-based channels for dissemination.

Around 2001-02, a broad-based consensus emerged that a "good" early warning system was one that: *(a)* is based "close to the ground" or has strong field-based networks of monitors; *(b)* uses multiple sources of information and both qualitative and quantitative analytical methods; *(c)* capitalises on appropriate communication and information technology; *(d)* provides regular reports and updates on conflict dynamics to key national and international stakeholders; and *(e)* has a strong link to responders or response mechanisms.

This understanding of good practice in early warning systems fed into the development of several inter-governmental initiatives, including the IGAD's CEWARN and ECOWAS's ECOWARN (2003-04). Beyond this good practice, some systems (*e.g.* CEWARN, WARN, and the Programme on Human Security and Co-Existence) started combining early warning and early response into one system (discussed further below). This was a key characteristic of the newer systems.

First, second and third generation systems

It is possible to chart the evolution of early warning systems in generations according to their location, organisation and purpose. Different generational systems meet different demands, institutional needs and mandates – which means that all serve important current needs.

- First generation systems of conflict early warning (mid- to late 1990s until today) are largely headquarter-based. They draw information from different sources and analyse it using a variety of qualitative and quantitative methods. Examples include the early form of the ICG (before regional offices were established), the GEDS research project, the conflict indicators model used by the European Commission, and the current German BMZ indicator-based system.

- Second generation systems (early 2000 onwards) have a stronger link to the field. Often incorporating networks of monitors operating in conflict areas, they analyse data using qualitative and quantitative methods, prepare a range of different reporting products, and often either provide recommendations or bring decision makers together to plan responses. Examples include the contemporary systems of ICG, EAWARN, and FAST.

- Third generation systems (2003 until today) are based in conflict areas. Organised along lines similar to second generation systems, they have stronger response links. Often, early warning information is used to de-escalate situations (*e.g.* by dispelling rumours. Field monitors also often serve as "first" responders to signs of violence. Networks of local/national responders are part of the system. Examples include the Programme on Human Security and Co-Existence in the Eastern Province of Sri Lanka (Foundation for Coexistence), FEWER-Eurasia, WARN, ECOWARN, CEWARN, and some corporate systems established by multinationals in conflict-affected regions.[4]

A more detailed discussion of these systems (categorised into governmental, inter-governmental and non-governmental systems) follows in the next chapter.

Analytical conclusions

Conflict early warning as a field of conflict prevention is today undergoing significant (and appropriate) scrutiny. What value does it have for conflict prevention as a whole? Do investments in early warning yield better results than investments in other preventive projects? Have early warning efforts helped prevent violent conflict? And perhaps most importantly, are we in a better position today to prevent the loss of life on the scale seen during the 1994 Rwandan genocide?

Critics point to inaccurate predictions, failure to foresee important events and inadequate linking of operational responses to early warning (Matveeva, 2006). Indeed, since the majority of early warning systems typically draw on open source information, this suggests that they cannot capture information about the plans of conflicting parties that determine when and where violence is to escalate. It is also often argued that a good analysis of conflict ultimately boils down to simple personal judgement and that the "bells and whistles" (graphs, local information networks, etc.) of some early warning systems add little value. Furthermore, from a donor perspective, the visible impacts of early warning are often seen as meagre and therefore less appealing than other interventions such as disarmament and security sector reform, which appear to have more obvious benefits. Indeed, at times early warning analyses can provide donor officials with political headaches, by being alarmist or offensive to other governments, or by advocating responses that are not feasible.

Proponents of conflict early warning say that it basically serves the same function today as it has for centuries in other fields: it helps decision makers and other stakeholders anticipate developments and understand the nature and dynamics of different situations (Lavoix, 2007). In its contemporary form, and at a minimum, conflict early warning contributes to the evidence base of conflict prevention decision making. Beyond that, a good early warning system (along with its information sources and analytical tools) helps anticipate trends in violent conflict situations. Those systems that have strong links to response, it is argued, provide options for conflict management and prevention, and forums for joint problem definition, response planning among different actors, and local responses to escalating situations.

However, despite advances made in policy integration, tools, methodologies and systems, we are now only marginally (if at all) in a better position to prevent situations of mass violence. Early response remains elusive and, of course, driven by political, institutional and operational considerations. Additional perspectives on these issues will be given throughout this paper. The final chapter revisits the value of conflict early warning and draws conclusions.

Notes

1. A global network of NGOs, United Nations agencies, and academic institutions focused on response-oriented early warning that was launched in 1997.

2. A West African network of civil society organisations working on conflict prevention and later early warning, established in 1997.

3. "Coding" here refers to the categorisation of information under different indicator headings.

4. Due to confidentiality issues, these third generation systems cannot be described here.

Chapter 2

The Range of Early Warning Tools and Systems

Conflict early warning is today trying to find a balance between remaining relevant to its funders and focusing on the protection and preservation of life. However, it is tilting significantly towards the former. The pursuit of relevance means that the notion of an open source, pro-people and pro-peace conflict early warning system is giving way to one with a far more pronounced intelligence dimension, particularly among governmental and inter-governmental agencies that run such systems. Whereas this is in part a consequence of changing perceptions of international threats in the north, it bodes badly for those who believe that conflict early warning can contribute to a more democratic peace, focused on human security.

An all-encompassing view of the early warning field will show tools and systems that cover, *inter alia,* natural disasters, famine and refugee flows. Although narrower, the scope of conflict early warning is also fairly broad: it includes tools and systems that seek to predict and prevent mass violence, violent conflict, war, genocide, human rights abuses, political instability, and state fragility. The focus here will be on tools/systems that deal with violent conflict and state fragility.[1]

It is important to stress that most conflict early warning tools and systems are designed to meet an expressed target audience need. These needs are institution- and context-specific as well as people-centred. Both the institutional framework and the context (*i.e.* the conflict environment) have changed substantially over the past 15-20 years.

- Institutionally, the past 15-20 years have seen important advances in international, regional and global capabilities to respond to conflict, both in terms of operational and structural initiatives.[2] Development agencies have been given a greater role in prevention, and conflict sensitivity has been mainstreamed among them. Geographically, stronger capabilities among regional organisations and civil society groups in early warning, preventive action and crisis management have added an important new target audience for early warning systems.

- Contextually, real and perceived threats to security have changed. From the end of the Cold War, the focus shifted in the 1990s to the prevention and resolution of intra-state conflicts. The 2001 September 11 attacks on the United States saw a dramatic shift of focus towards counterterrorism and counter-proliferation of weapons of mass destruction. The complexities and fallout of the wars in Afghanistan and Iraq, organised crime, drugs and human trafficking, and mass migration are now high on regional and international agendas, along with a more explicit focus on the capabilities of individual states to manage these.

At a more technical level, a review of conflict early warning systems has to start with an understanding of the evolution and range of different analytical tools and methods. Without these different tools and methods, early warning systems would be simple information gathering entities with no analytical capability. The sections below, therefore, discuss quantitative and qualitative tools and methods for analysis of violent conflict and state fragility, before reviewing existing early warning systems in governmental, inter-governmental and non-governmental organisations.

The tools and methods

Overview

The evolution of the conflict early warning field has been driven by the advances made in quantitative and qualitative analytical tools. As the capabilities and value of these tools grew, they were integrated into the different early warning systems operated by governments, inter-governmental organisations and NGOs. The sections below look at the range of quantitative and qualitative analytical tools available, discuss their approaches and applications, and assess their strengths and weaknesses.

The number-crunchers … quantitative tools and methods

As mentioned above, quantitative conflict analysis tools emerged in the 1990s. Quantitative indices for state fragility (see Table 2.1) came into view roughly from 2000 onwards. Fundamentally, the empirical research that has gone into the development of these tools and indices has contributed significantly to our understanding of causal relationships in violent conflict and state fragility. A number of scholars suggest that some of these models now demonstrate high predictive accuracy (80%+) and to that extent are an important contribution to the field (Goldstone, 2008).

Table 2.1. **Quantitative models/methods/systems – violent conflict and state fragility**

Violent conflict	
Leiden University (Netherlands): Inter-Disciplinary Research Programme on Root Causes of Human Rights Violations	Kansas University (United States): Protocol for the Assessment of Non-violent Direct Action (PANDA); Kansas Events Data System (KEDS)
Georgia Institute of Technology (United States): Conflict Early Warning Project – Pattern Recognition	Fein (United States): Life Integrity Violations Analysis (LIVA)
Carleton University (Canada): Country Indicators for Foreign Policy (CIFP)	Virtual Research Associates (United States): GeoMonitor
Economist Intelligence Unit (United Kingdom): The Global Peace Index	US Naval Academy (United States): State Failure Project; Accelerators of Genocide Project
State fragility	
The Fund for Peace (United States): Failed States Index (annual)[3]	University of Maryland/Centre for International Development and Conflict Management (United States): Peace and Conflict Instability Ledger (annual)
George Mason University (United States): State Fragility Index (annual)	Center for Global Development (United States): Engaging Fragile States
Political Instability Task Force (United States): Internal Wars and Failures of Governance 1955-2006	Center for Systemic Peace (United States): Polity IV, Coups d'Etat, PITF Problem Set
Carleton University (Canada): Country Indicators for Foreign Policy (CIFP)	Institute for State Effectiveness (United States): Sovereignty Index
United Agency for International Development (United States): Measuring State Fragility	

The development of these tools and methods (particularly forecasting models) involves "training algorithms on historical data, usually examining several decades in the post-World War II era, to arrive at factors [with most predictive significance]" (Goldstone, 2008). Goldstone and others also distinguish between quantitative forecasting models (that use a discrete set of variables for predicting crisis and conflict in any given country) and structural analogies (methods based on key similarities across a set of countries). Most of the models developed over the years to predict (or assess risk of) violent conflict and state fragility can be categorised as either one or the other.

The purpose of quantitative conflict analysis methods has largely been to predict or assess the risk of violent conflict. The models are indicator-based and data are collected for indicators as the basis of analysis. Data used are in some cases structural (*e.g.* poverty data) or events-based (*e.g.* actions by different parties), or both.

An early challenge encountered by quantitative methods to predict or monitor violent conflict was how to use and code the available information for purposes of analysis. This was particularly challenging for models designed to monitor evolving conflict situations for early warning purposes (*e.g.* KEDS). It was less of an issue for those initiatives (*e.g.* CIFP) that drew heavily on less dynamic data sets to determine risk of conflict. The challenge was increased as sources of data for these pre- and actual conflict situations were limited. A statistically significant number of events is required to identify trends. For example, the Conflict and Co-operation Model (used by VRA and FAST) (see Box 2.1 and Figure 2.1) requires ideally one to two reported events per day for useful trends to be drawn. If media sources only were used, studies of pre-crisis situations would have (often too) few reports to draw from. (Local reporting in newspapers might help but these are not online and not translated.) FAST's use of field monitors was therefore a step in the right direction. Nevertheless, their attempt to "use FAST data to produce forecasts largely failed due to data quality and the lack of coded events" (Schmeidl, 2008). Global news feeds that provide easy access to and monitoring of millions of news clippings have addressed some (but far from all) of these challenges (Hopkins and King, 2008).

Box 2.1. **Basic theory behind Goldstein's conflict and co-operation model**

Average Domestic Co-operation – The Goldstein Average Domestic Co-operation indicator displays the cumulative average of the positive (Goldstein) values of all co-operative intra-state or domestic events in a specific period (means the sum of the positive Goldstein values divided by the total number of cooperative domestic events).

Average Domestic Conflict – The Goldstein Average Domestic Conflict indicator displays the cumulative average of the negative (Goldstein) values of all conflictive intra-state or domestic events in a specific period (means the sum of the negative Goldstein values divided by the total number of conflictive domestic events). For interpretation purposes we take the absolute values (means positive values).

Source: Adapted from FEWER-Eurasia (2005), "Strategic Reconstruction and Development Assessment – North Caucasus".

Figure 2.1. **Average domestic conflict and co-operation graph**

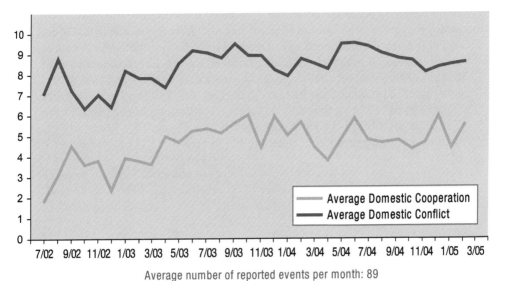

Average number of reported events per month: 89

Source: swisspeace (2005), "FAST Update: Russian Federation/Chechnya", Semi-annual Risk Assessment, November 2004 to February 2005.

In the example for Chechnya (Figure 2.1), two lines (grey [the top line] and dark black [the bottom line]) indicate trends in "conflict events" and "co-operation events", respectively, over two years. The assumption is that violence is likely to erupt when the number of "conflict events" increases and the number of "co-operation events" decreases. Visually, that happens when the top grey curve goes up at the same time as the bottom dark black curve goes down. However, in order to draw part of the line each month, a certain number of "co-operation events" or "conflict events" are needed. The challenge of managing data was overcome with advances in automated coding and the use (by FAST) of local monitors for data collection.

Quantitative models are also used to monitor state fragility or to assess the risk of state collapse. Also indicator-based, most of these models present a "risk score" and ranking for different countries, often displayed in indices. For example, the PITF uses four indicators (or variables) to predict political crisis, including regime type, infant mortality, the presence or absence of high levels of discrimination, and number of neighbouring countries that experience violent conflict (Goldstone, 2008).

As with conflict analysis methods, there are data challenges. For models focused on prediction within an 18-24-month period, annual data are often not adjusted in real time (it arrives late), data may be inaccurate, and for some countries data may be sparse. Indices of state fragility can be used by policy makers to prioritise countries at risk and draw up "watch lists". More difficult is the use of state fragility methods to inform programming, as this requires a deeper understanding of specific contexts – although more recent indices distinguish between various dimensions of fragility and thus give a more nuanced picture than just an aggregated list. This may provide entry points for policy, programming and resource allocation. An example from The Fund for Peace Failed States Index (see Figure 2.2.) illustrates the priority-setting application of state fragility indices.

Figure 2.2. **Failed States Index Score 2007**

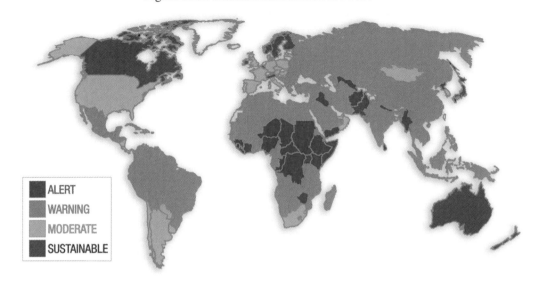

Source: The Fund for Peace.

There are several strengths of quantitative tools and methods:

- Their predictive capacity, particularly related to political crisis and instability, is high (80+% with some models, such as PITF).

- Their immediate policy value, in terms priority setting and "watch listing" is significant. The visuals provided (maps, country lists) are easily understood.

- Models that draw on a larger number of indicators (*e.g.* CIFP and The Fund for Peace) may also provide pointers for programming.

Some of the weaknesses, particularly in relation to data, have been discussed above. In addition, the following should be noted:

- As explained by Goldstone (2008), even the best quantitative models will at times have reduced predictive value, as they "cannot reflect all possible interactions or added effects with factors that are specific to individual countries at a certain time."

- The graphs, charts, country lists etc. in themselves provide decision makers with little insight into what is happening on the ground or what needs to be done. The fact base of quantitative models provide too little context for guidance on decision making. Moreover, decision makers often perceive these models as black boxes and may be reluctant to place their trust in complex mathematical tools that they do not understand (Campbell and Meier, 2007).

- The majority of forecasts made are rarely assessed for accuracy. As Taleb (2007) pointedly notes, "out of close to a million papers published in politics, finance and economics, there have only been a small number of checks on the predictive quality of such knowledge." Furthermore, high accuracy measures alone are not sufficient. One must consider precision and recall as well as the number of false positives and false negatives generated for each forecast.

- Quantitative models for conflict forecasting should inform appropriately targeted preventive measures. However, many models identify conflict-risk factors that are not susceptible to external influence, such as ideology of ruling élite, autocracy, and ethnic minority ruling élite. As Woocher (2007) rightly remarks, "short of coercive regime change, policy-makers lack the tools to influence these factors, particularly in a reasonably short time frame."

The strengths and weaknesses of these models have led analysts and early warners to combine methods – quantitative, qualitative, and mixed quantitative models. Such a triangulation of methods (and sources) has been attempted by several systems, including FAST and CEWARN.

The qualifiers – qualitative tools for analysis and response

Qualitative methods for conflict analysis first emerged in the second half of the 1990s and responded to a need for tools that would enable a better understanding of violent conflict and how to respond. From that point of departure, different development agencies (especially DFID) further advanced these methods to inform how programmes and projects should be adapted in conflict situations. Around the same time, the planning potential of conflict analysis tools was bolstered through the work of GTZ, FEWER/International Alert/Saferworld and others that linked analysis to different planning frameworks. The need for tools to evaluate the impact of different interventions in violent conflict situations led to the development of Peace and Conflict Impact Assessment (PCIA) methods (CPR Network, etc.). The most recent step in the evolution of qualitative conflict analysis tools was taken by UNDP (Bureau for Crisis Prevention and Recovery and UNDP/Indonesia) with the development of a multi-stakeholder analysis/planning process that helps build a shared vision and understanding of obstacles to peace among conflicting parties. In essence, these "Peace and Development Analysis" (PDA) processes use conflict analysis as a tool for response (*i.e.* trust building, consensus building) – particularly in post conflict settings (Indonesia, Fiji, etc.).

The qualitative methods developed for state fragility situations are very recent (since 2005). They capitalise on lessons learned and best practice in conflict analysis to make the immediate link from analysis to planning and strategising. Unlike some of the early qualitative conflict analysis tools that were quite theoretical in nature, current state fragility tools seek immediate operational relevance. For example, the Dutch "Stability Assessment Framework: Designing Integrated Responses for Security, Governance and Development" (2005) not only provides an analytical and strategic framework, but also outlines the required practical process for the preparation of a Stability Assessment Framework. See Table 2.2 for an overview of tools surveyed.

Qualitative tools were integrated into different early warning systems as they evolved. The target audience, for example, of the FEWER analytical methodology was its civil society early warning network members. The use of these qualitative tools was complemented by drawing on quantitative methods to bolster the rigour of analysis, for example in the FAST, ECOWARN, and CEWARN systems. In order to help provide options for response, many early warning systems also draw on analytical methods with strong planning elements. Others have also integrated PCIA concepts into their monitoring, examining how different responses contribute to an improvement or deterioration of violent conflict situations.

As with quantitative tools, qualitative methods are peppered with much (and often confusing) jargon that sometimes conceals the simple thinking behind them. A PCIA tool, for example, basically involves using the findings from a conflict analysis and a project/programme document to answer two questions: *(a)* what is the impact of a conflict on a project/programme? and *(b)* what is the impact of a project/programme on a conflict? Through interviews, observations, data collection and combining conflict analysis with a "nuts and bolts" review of a given project/programme a judgement is formed of (past, present or future) impacts.

The operational value of qualitative methods is relatively high, particularly for development agencies that implement projects/programmes in conflict-affected regions. In fact, respondents from development agencies indicate that qualitative tools serve their purposes better than early warning systems. This is probably due to the easy fit with planning cycles, and the useful applications of these tools to planning and evaluation. Qualitative methods also tend to be more consistent with a participatory approach, which many field-based agencies already take.

Table 2.2. **Qualitative models/methods – violent conflict and state fragility**

Violent conflict	
Conflict Prevention and Post-Conflict Reconstruction (CPR) Network: Early Warning and Early Response Handbook (V2.3) (2005); Peace and Conflict Impact Assessment Handbook (V2.2) (2005); *Guide de Diagnostic des Conflits* (2003)	United States Agency for International Development (United States): Conflict Assessment Framework (2005); Conducting a Conflict Assessment: A Framework for Strategy and Program Development (2004)
Bush: A Handbook for Peace and Conflict Impact Assessment (2004)	UNDP: Conflict-Related Development Analysis (2002); Peace and Development Analysis (2003)
Department for International Development (United Kingdom): Conducting Strategic Conflict Assessments (2002)	World Bank: Conflict Analysis Framework (2002)
Deutsche Gesellschaft für Technische Zusammenarbeit (Germany): Conflict Analysis for Project Planning and Management (2001)	Forum on Early Warning and Early Response (United Kingdom): Conflict Analysis and Response Definition (2001)
FEWER, International Alert, Saferworld (United Kingdom): Development in Conflict: A Seven Step Tool for Planners (2001)	CARE International (United States): Benefits-Harms Handbook (2001)
Clingendael Institute (Netherlands): Conflict and Policy Assessment Framework (2000)	European Commission: Check-List for Root Causes of Conflict (1999); Peace-building and Conflict Prevention in Developing Countries : A Practical Guide (1999); Peace and Conflict Impact Assessment: A Practical Working Tool for Prioritising Development Assistance in Unstable Situations (1999)
German Federal Ministry for Economic Cooperation and Development (BMZ): An Indicator Model for Use as an Additional Instrument for Planning and Analysis in Development Co-operation (1998)	Forum on Early Warning and Early Response (United Kingdom): A Manual for Early Warning and Early Response (1998)
The Fund for Peace (United States): Conflict Assessment System Tool (1996)	
State fragility	
Canadian International Development Agency (Canada): On the Road to Recovery: Breaking the Cycle of Poverty and Fragility: A Guide for Effective Development Cooperation in Fragile States (2007)	Department for International Development (United Kingdom): Scenario and Contingency Planning for Fragile States (2007); Country Governance Analysis (2006); Drivers of Change (2003)
Netherlands Ministry of Foreign Affairs (Netherlands): The Stability Assessment Framework: Designing Integrated Responses for Security, Governance and Development (2005)	Prime Minister's Strategy Unit (United Kingdom): Countries at Risk of Instability: Country Strategy Formulation Process Manual (2005)

The strengths of qualitative methods for analysis of violent conflict and state fragility (when applied well) are as follows:

- They provide rich contextual information and analysis that can be simple enough for desk officers to absorb and do something with.

- They often have strong built-in applications to planning and evaluation that help agencies plan and improve projects and programmes.

- They include stakeholders more directly and provide for two-way interaction.

However, they also have significant weaknesses. Qualitative analyses:

- Are often one-off snapshots of rapidly evolving situations. They are quickly outdated.

- Sometimes oversimplify the complexity of violent conflict and state fragility situations (similar to quantitative methods). By doing so, they may mislead and badly inform policy makers and other stakeholders.

- Usually proffer technical solutions to complex political issues. They implicitly may suggest that technocratic approaches can replace required political action.

- Are fundamentally based on personal judgement. If the analyst is unfamiliar with the situation, the likelihood of a poor analysis is significant.

- Vary greatly in how rigorously they are carried out and how reliable they are. In addition, comparing extensive textual analysis is more taxing than comparing quantitative results that can be rendered visually.

- Are subject to the same data restrictions and challenges as quantitative methods. Poor or incomplete data lead to bad analysis.

Preliminary conclusions – much progress, but weaknesses remain

Significant advances have been made in quantitative and qualitative analytical tools for violent conflict and state fragility. Quantitative methods have strong predictive capabilities, particularly in relation to political crisis and instability. State fragility indices provide easily graspable "watch lists" and help agencies working on these issues to prioritise focus countries. Qualitative methods provide rich context analysis, as well as ways to plan programmatic responses and assess the impact of these responses on violent conflicts. The more recent qualitative methods for state fragility analysis can provide useful planning frameworks for programmatic responses but are not yet widely used in agencies, and more work is required to refine them. Qualitative tools satisfy important analytical requirements among development agencies – particularly in terms of informing programming. Numerous weaknesses persist, nonetheless. Analytical tools fundamentally oversimplify complex and fluid violent conflicts and situations of state fragility. They provide simple snapshots that are quickly outdated, and the quality of analysis suffers from data deficits that characterise many countries affected by conflict and state fragility.

The operational early warning systems

Overview

Early warning can broadly mean the collection of information to understand and pre-empt future developments. For the purposes of this report, a more restrictive definition has been applied where *"early warning systems are those that involve regular and organised collection and analysis of open source information on violent conflict situations. They deliver a set of early warning products (based on qualitative and/or quantitative conflict analysis methods) that are linked to response instruments/mechanisms."* However, in order to show the breadth of existing systems, the definition was used more for guidance than for strict selection purposes. Respondents were asked a set of questions on the focus, funding, activities, methodology, etc. of their early warning systems (see Box 2.2). The surveyed conflict early warning systems are listed in Table 2.3.

Governmental early warning systems

Most OECD DAC members and governments surveyed do not have what can be defined as a conflict early warning system. "Early warnings" come through either intelligence services, diplomatic missions in affected countries, or inter-governmental and non-governmental early warning systems. Those that do have early warning systems in place include France, Germany, and the United States. Depending on their purpose and institutional location, these may or may not have a link to national intelligence services.

Box 2.2. **Survey questions on early warning systems**

1. What is the operational and geographic focus of your early warning system?

2. What is the annual budget for your early warning system and who provides the funding?

3. What are the main activities (monitoring, briefings, report writing, etc.) of the early warning system?

4. What methodology is used (qualitative and/or quantitative – conflict analysis, state fragility, etc.), and what are the main information sources (media, local monitors, structural data, etc.) of your early warning system?

5. Who is your target audience (decision makers in particular agencies, local communities, general public, etc.) and what warning products (reports, briefs, documentaries, etc.) and frequency of these do you offer? Is there a feedback loop between yourself and the target audience?

6. What are the linkages between your early warning system and early response? Does it provide recommendations for response? Is there a direct connection to specific mechanisms/instruments?

7. If your early warning system co-operates, co-ordinates activities, or operates in partnership with any other external agencies (governments, multilaterals, NGOs, etc.), which agencies are these and what are the forms of co-operation/co-ordination/partnership?

8. What do you see as the main strengths and limitations/challenges faced by your early warning system?

9. Are there any success stories or particular impacts that your early warning system has been responsible for?

Table 2.3. **Governmental, inter-governmental, and non-governmental early warning systems**

Governmental early warning systems	Inter-governmental early warning systems	Non-governmental early warning systems
Secrétariat Général de la Défense Nationale (France): *Système d'Alerte Précoce* (SAP)	United Nations: OCHA – Early Warning Unit; Humanitarian Situation Room (Colombia) UNDP – Country-level early warning systems in Ghana, Kenya, Ukraine (Crimea), Bolivia (PAPEP), Balkans, Kyrgyzstan	FEWER-Eurasia (Russia): FEWER-Eurasia Network
		ISS (South Africa): Early Warning System
German Federal Ministry for Economic Cooperation and Development (BMZ): Crisis Early Warning System	EU: EU Watch List	swisspeace (Switzerland): Early Recognition and Analysis of Tensions (FAST)
United States Government: Office of the Coordinator for Reconstruction and Stabilization and National Intelligence Council: Instability Watch List	AU: Continental Early Warning System (CEWS)	Russian Academy of Sciences (Moscow): Network for Ethnological Monitoring and Early Warning (EAWRN)
	CEEAC: Mechanisme d'Alerte Rapide pour l'Afrique Centrale (MARAC)	Foundation for Tolerance International (Kyrgyzstan): Early Warning for Violence Prevention Project
	ECOWAS: ECOWAS Early Warning and Early Response Network (ECOWARN)	Crisis Group (Belgium): Crisis Watch
	IGAD: Conflict Early Warning and Response Mechanism (CEWARN)	Foundation for Co-Existence (Sri Lanka): Program on Human Security and Co-Existence
	OSCE: Centre for Conflict Prevention	West Africa Network for Peacebuilding (Ghana): Early Warning and Response Network (WARN)
		FEWER-Africa (Kenya): Ituri Watch (Democratic Republic of Congo)

The purpose of most governmental early warning systems is to identify and assess threats to national interests and/or to inform crisis prevention and peacebuilding programmes. Purpose dictates the institutional set-up and methodology used.

France's *Système d'Alerte Précoce* (SAP) and the US National Intelligence Office for Warning pay particular attention to threats posed by crises to national interests. The French system is located in the *Secrétariat Général de la Défense Nationale*. The US system is located in the Office of the Coordinator for Reconstruction and Stabilization (State Department) and National Intelligence Council. The French system uses a qualitative method and generates monthly update reports on key indicators, while the US system generates a "watch list" that draws heavily on quantitative analysis. Both systems draw on open source and classified information for their analyses.

The German early warning system is used to inform the crisis prevention and peacebuilding programmes of the Ministry for Economic Cooperation and Development (BMZ). Methodologically, it uses a qualitative indicator-based questionnaire, which has a quantitative scoring system attached to it. Each year, an assessment using this methodology is conducted by independent consultants of the German Institute for Global Area Studies (GIGA) on behalf of BMZ. Emerging results are reviewed and revised by BMZ country desks to arrive at a final listing of priority countries and directions for preventive programming.

The target audiences for all governmental systems are internal, and involve different levels of decision makers. Assessments are not usually publicly available. It is therefore not possible to pass judgment on the quality of analyses made or their value as an evidence base for decision makers.

The value added of governmental early warning systems, as stated by respondents, is twofold for the clients they serve:

- A crisis prediction capacity that enables proactive decision making, and a stronger basis for evidence-based decision making on countries affected by crisis.

- Improved programming through systematic country reviews and expert analysis.

The main challenge reported by governmental early warners is about catalysing response. The receptivity of decision makers in charge of responses is frequently limited.

Inter-governmental early warning systems

A number of inter-governmental organisations (particularly in Africa) have established conflict early warning systems. Broadly speaking, the purpose of these systems is to bolster the different organisations' ability to anticipate crises and initiate preventive measures. Among some of the regional organisations (OSCE, AU, IGAD, ECOWAS, ECCAS), the geographical scope is limited to member countries (see Figure 2.3). The EU has a global remit for the work carried out by the Council's Policy Planning and Early Warning Unit, as does the United Nation's Humanitarian Situation Room. Most surveys of early warning systems will also include SADC on their list. Although some governmental systems have been included despite their intelligence links, the SADC approach is more formalised intelligence sharing than early warning – and therefore has been excluded.

Figure 2.3. **Early warning systems in the European region**

Source: INCAS Consulting Ltd. and Urban Guru Ltd. (United Kingdom).

Among the African regional organisations, IGAD's CEWARN and the ECOWAS ECOWARN system are the most developed. The AU's CEWS is making progress, and ECCAS's MARAC is under development. Together, these systems cover a range of issues and countries in Africa (see Figure 2.4.). Most of the inter-governmental systems in Africa involve some form of co-operation with civil society organisations, which in turn broadens their access to information and analysis.

In many cases, these systems apply a mix of quantitative and qualitative methods – all indicator-based. They use largely (with some exceptions) open source information and information collected by "local" monitors to produce different products (policy briefs, baseline reports, thematic reports, alerts, etc.) for institutional decision makers. Beyond the delivery of warning reports to decision makers, established links between these early warning and response systems remain mostly unclear. With the exception of CEWARN, no formalised protocols were identified that integrate early warning reporting within decision-making systems for response.

Figure 2.4. **Early warning systems in the African region**

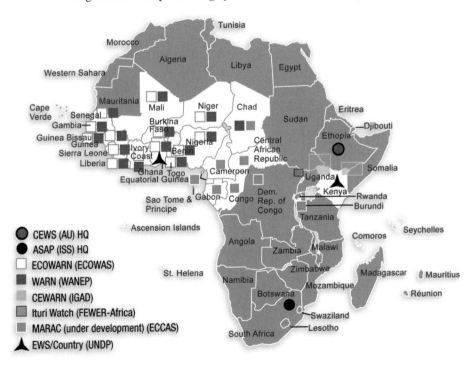

Source: INCAS Consulting and Urban Guru Ltd. (United Kingdom).

Several inter-governmental organisations operate early warning systems that are practically global. The EU, for example, has both a watch list (updated twice a year by civilian and military analysts from the Council, EUSITCEN, Commission and EU member states) and a Policy Planning and Early Warning Unit (PPEWU) which is located in the Council and engages in early warning analysis. Within the United Nations there are several early warning approaches, including the Humanitarian Situation Room, the Framework Team, and agency-led country-level systems in different parts of the world.

- The EU uses open source information, "grey information" from EU Delegations and member states, and GIS data from the EUSITCEN to generate its watch list and other analyses prepared by the PPEWU. Its target audience includes Commission and Council decision makers and staff, as well as representatives of member states.

- The UN early warning systems are open source, especially those operational at the country level. In New York, the Framework Team meets regularly to discuss countries of concern, share analyses, and formulate inter-agency responses to emerging and/or ongoing crisis situations.

The value added of inter-governmental early warning systems is the evidence base it provides for decision making and the priority-setting contribution of watch list products. These systems help inform debates on responses to violence and instability in different countries. Interviewees also stress that a shared problem definition on crisis-affected countries or regions sets the stage for more coherent interdepartmental/agency responses.

There are numerous challenges faced by inter-governmental early warning systems. These include:

- Member state sensitivities on monitoring of violent conflict and state fragility, as well as the labelling of a country as "conflict prone" or a "fragile state". The work of regional organisations and the United Nations is particularly restricted by such sensitivities.

- Political interference and manipulation of analyses prepared is a consequence of the sensitivities of member states when inter-governmental organisations engage in early warning work.

- Restrictions on early warning system coverage affect several inter-governmental organisations. Such restrictions mean that only certain topics (humanitarian issues, pastoral conflicts, etc.) can be covered and that allocations for early warning efforts are controlled.

- As with some other systems, inter-governmental systems are hierarchical. The flow of information is one-way, from field to headquarters. The analysis is rarely shared with those who need it the most, *i.e.* the at-risk communities themselves.

- Several interviewees have pointed to the difficulty in linking inter-governmental early warning efforts to high-level political and security responses. Part of this difficulty is related to a lack of conviction among higher-level decision makers about the value of early warning.

Non-governmental systems

Non-governmental early warning systems differ in purpose and organisation. Some are focused on providing early warning analysis to inform decision making on conflict situations without recommendations for response, while others provide recommendations, engage in advocacy, or are engaged in response activities themselves. In terms of organisation, most non-governmental early warning systems deploy staff or local networks in or close to conflict-affected areas. Where local monitors are used, they will report according to standard formats and the information collected feeds into analyses.

For the most part (with the exception of the International Crisis Group), the analytical methodologies of these groups are clear. Several non-governmental systems (*e.g.* FEWER-Eurasia, Program on Human Security and Co-Existence) use both qualitative and quantitative methods for analysis, as championed by FEWER and the former swisspeace FAST system. Non-governmental systems use exclusively open source information and information provided by local monitors. Based on these methods and the information collected, different products are generated, including briefs, baseline reports, documentaries, briefings, updates and thematic reports.

Early warning systems with a global outlook included FEWER, FAST (both now closed due to funding problems) and the ICG. At a regional level, WANEP/WARN and ISS cover the ECOWAS region and crisis countries in Africa, respectively; FEWER-Eurasia and EAWARN cover the North Caucasus. At a country level, Ituri-Watch (FEWER-Africa) covers Ituri in the DR Congo, while the Foundation for Co-Existence (Sri Lanka) covers the Eastern Province in Sri Lanka and Sri Lanka more broadly. The most recent initiatives include the early warning project managed by the Foundation for Tolerance International that covers Kyrgyzstan, the Belun/CICR early warning project in Timor-Leste (EWER), the Tribal

Liaison Office (TLO) community-based project in South Afghanistan and the Ushahidi system for Kenya (see Figure 2.5).

Fundamental to the non-governmental approach to early warning is a belief that integrated multi-stakeholder responses to violent conflict and political instability are most effective. This is why such systems make their reports broadly available and, in some cases, bring different organisations together to plan joint response strategies. However, the inability to catalyse responses has led several systems (defined as "third generation systems" above) to set up their own response mechanisms and instruments in order to deal with micro-level violence.

Figure 2.5. **Early warning systems in the Asian region**

Source: INCAS Consulting Ltd. and Urban Guru Ltd. (United Kingdom).

This has included the development of systems that aim to empower local at-risk communities directly to manage violent conflict and/or to get out of harm's way. These community-based systems focus on training vulnerable populations with explicitly nonviolent tactics including conflict management skills and conflict preparedness. As such these systems balance an emphasis on prevention with a focus on preparedness to react to the possible failure to prevent conflict.

The value added of non-governmental early warning is in broadening and deepening the evidence base for decision makers on violent conflict situations and state fragility – broadening in terms of the range of information sources (beyond diplomatic cables, media sources, intelligence reports) and deepening in terms of proximity to communities (beyond macro-level reports, etc.). Non-governmental and community-based early warning is also less constrained by political sensitivities than inter-governmental systems, particularly when it comes to statements made, issues covered, dissemination, intervention and sovereignty issues. Non-governmental and community-based systems that are more involved on the response side are in some cases able to convene different actors to plan joint responses, or implement micro-level responses themselves.

Non-governmental systems have multiple vulnerabilities. For example, if these systems issue reports on sensitive matters (particularly related to the political economy of conflicts or controversial international policies of major powers), safety of staff may be compromised and the funding base may be affected. At the same time, with few exceptions, most of these initiatives are in any case chronically underfunded. In practice, this means that their ability to maintain analysts and information networks, both essential for "good" early warning is constrained.

Wired to the bulb? The warning-response link

The warning-response link is often discussed in terms of whether early warning is "wired" to early response – the same way as a plug (early warning) is wired to a bulb (response). Good early warning should be compelling enough to catalyse response. There are not many success stories attesting to how early warning has done this. A few are given throughout this report: a number of respondents did indeed identify situations where early warning yielded different and effective responses. Examples that should be researched and documented further include:

- ECOWARN success in averting crisis in Guinea and Togo through regular warning reports and strong links with response mechanisms.

- Ituri Watch prevention of clashes between communities in the DR Congo through use of early warnings to catalyse local responses.

- The Early Warning for Violence Prevention Project (Foundation for Tolerance International) alerted the Kazakh parliament and government about potential conflicts along the Kygryz-Kazakh (Talas oblast in Kyrgyzstan) that led to preventive action.

- FEWER-Eurasia contributed to the decrease in the number of disappearances in Chechnya through monitoring and humanitarian dialogue.

Among the success stories most often quoted in the annals of early warning is that of the OSCE's early warning of the crisis in the former Yugoslav Republic of Macedonia (see Case Study 1 in Box 2.3).

Box 2.3. **Case Study 1: The OSCE's early warning about the former Yugoslav Republic of Macedonia**

In the late 1990s the OSCE High Commissioner on National Minorities, Mr Van der Stoel, had closely followed the relationship between the ethnic Macedonian majority and the ethnic Albanian minority in the former Yugoslav Republic of Macedonia. His work was supported by the OSCE Spillover Monitor Mission to Skopje, which dealt with the effects of the conflict in Kosovo.

Mr Van der Stoel enjoyed a high degree of confidence of both parties thanks to a long-term, balanced and highly professional involvement in regional inter-ethnic relations. He dealt with several root causes of the conflict, including linguistic rights, education, media, participation of minorities in public life, etc. He was instrumental in establishing the Albanian language Tetovo University, with donations of EUR 5 million by the government of the Netherlands and the European Commission.

As ethnic tension grew in late 2000 and early 2001 and the likelihood of a more violent armed conflict grew, Mr Van der Stoel issued repeated early warnings, including a dramatic statement at the meeting of the OSCE Permanent Council.

Acting upon these early warnings, in late March 2001 the OSCE Chairman in Office appointed Ambassador Robert Frowick as Personal Envoy to the FYROM. On 1 July 2001 the Chairman in Office appointed Mr Van der Stoel as Personal Envoy, asking him to "facilitate dialogue and provide advice for a speedy solution to the current crisis".

Simultaneously, the OSCE conducted intensive co-ordination and soon engaged in close co-operation with NATO, the European Union and later the Council of Europe.

Through this co-ordinated action the crisis was contained and stability and peace was gradually restored.

Source: Marton Krasznai (UNECE, formerly OSCE).

Is the lack of early response a consequence of "poor" early warning? The answer is yes, partly. A review of the many early warning reports produced by different organisations does raise important questions about depth and quality of analysis. It is also clear that, due to a host of sensitivities and the overall "murky" nature of violent conflict, much of the hidden political economy of violent conflict remains unassessed. Publishing information and analysis on this carries great personal risk, both physically and in terms of reputation. Yet such information and analysis is critical for informed responses to violent conflict. So despite some of the reported and claimed successes, there is much scope for improvement – but improvement needs funding.

Preliminary conclusions – how mature is the field?

Early warning systems now exist within governments, multilateral agencies and NGOs. They play different roles, ranging from giving alerts and catalysing response to bolstering the evidence base of decision making, to serving as response mechanisms themselves. There is consensus on what constitutes a "good" early warning system, and this good practice has been put into operation in initiatives such as FAST, FEWER-Eurasia, CEWARN, and ECOWARN to mention just a few (see Box 2.4). The field, however, suffers from under-investment, as illustrated in the closure of FAST (see Box 2.5 for discussion). There are also serious questions about the quality of analysis produced by many early warning systems. Do they really cover the real issues? Is the analytical depth sufficient for decision making? The answer to these questions is probably no. There is a great need to bolster analytical rigour.

Box 2.4. **Good practice in operational conflict early warning systems**

A "good" early warning system is one that:

- Is based "close to the ground" or has strong field-based networks of monitors.

- Uses multiple sources of information and both qualitative/quantitative analytical methods.

- Capitalises on appropriate communication and information technology.

- Provides regular reports and updates on conflict dynamics to key national and international stakeholders.

- Has a strong link to responders or response mechanisms.

Box 2.5. **Lessons from the closure of FAST**

In April 2008, the FAST early warning system closed its doors after a decade of operations, and four years after the closure of FEWER. FAST was recognised by most practitioners as the embodiment of good early warning practice. It was a system that combined qualitative and quantitative analytical methods, and worked with civil society groups in the countries it covered to gain field-level information through local information networks. Its reports, the FAST updates, risk assessments, trends, etc. had a broad readership beyond its main funder, Swiss Agency for Development Cooperation. So why, after ten years of successful work, did FAST close?

Interviews and discussions with FAST staff, donors, and other practitioners proffered the following explanations:

- A birth defect of FAST and some other early warning initiatives is their alignment with development agencies – as natural partners and donors. These agencies benefit more from conflict assessment methodologies than from early warning reports when it comes to informing their programming. Early warning does not present value added for them.

- The main clients of FAST reports were in foreign ministries, security agencies, regional organisations, etc.; they dealt more with operational than structural prevention. However, they did not pay for it. Often, the budgets for FAST were in development agencies, which sometimes felt that FAST analyses were too superficial (Schmeidl, 2008).

- Unlike the ICG, FAST was not able to establish high-level relationships with political leaders in donor countries. Rather, working relationships were with mid-level staff in different ministries. Regular turnover of staff meant that early warning had to be "sold again and again" – and such efforts were not always successful.

With the closure of FAST and FEWER, the only remaining "global" provider of analyses (beyond regional and national early warning systems) is the ICG. ICG is a well-run organisation and its reports are often of high quality. Nonetheless, its constituency and methodology are still unclear. It remains also to be seen whether reliance on one external provider of information and analysis is beneficial for international and regional decision makers.

Analytical conclusions

Conflict analysis tools and early warning systems have evolved significantly over the past decade. There is consensus on methodological and system good practice. This good practice has in turn fed into qualitative methods for response planning in fragile states.

As to quantitative and qualitative analytical tools, two conclusions can be drawn. First, there is no "best methodology" or "best set of indicators". There is basic good practice in quantitative and qualitative analysis and a range of methods draw on this. These are designed to serve the interests of their target institution. Second, the best approach is to combine quantitative and qualitative tools, and sometimes to combine different sets of quantitative methods (Goldstone, 2008). This ensures the necessary triangulation required for creating a robust evidence base for decision making.

At a systems level, good practice is clear and has been outlined above. There is also more clarity today about the value added of early warning systems, based on their application. To summarise, early warning systems provide:

- A crisis prediction capacity that enables proactive decision making.

- A stronger basis for evidence-based decision making on countries affected by crisis.

- Improved programming through systematic country reviews and expert analysis.

- A priority-setting contribution through watch list-type products.

- A starting point for developing a shared problem definition of crisis-affected countries that sets the stage for more coherent responses.

- An ideas pool for responses, and sometimes the forum to meet fellow responders and plan joint response strategies.

Having said this, it is clear that conflict and state fragility analyses serve the needs of development agencies better than early warning systems do. This is because conflict and state fragility assessments provide more institution-specific recommendations for programming than what comes from early warning systems. The more natural client for early warning systems is political decision-making institutions.

However, the poor quality of analyses, unrealistic recommendations, and biased or ungrounded opinions present in many early warning products means that "poor early warning" still remains an important cause of non-response to violent conflict.

Notes

1. See the accompanying *Compendium of Surveyed Early Warning Systems and Early Response Mechanisms/Instruments* in the annex for profiles of systems covered.

2. As explained in the Carnegie Commission on Preventing Deadly Conflict's (1997) report, operational prevention refers to "measures applicable in the face of immediate crisis", while structural prevention refers to "measures to ensure that crises do not arise in the first place or, if they do, that they do not recur."

3. While the Failed States Index represents its findings in a quantitative form, it uses multiple methods (i.e. quantitative and qualitative) to derive country scores. In addition, it also publishes brief country profiles in narrative form to explain the events and trends that drove the scores.

Chapter 3

Is Early Early? A Review of Response Mechanisms and Instruments

Advances over the past 15 years or so in early and rapid response have been made in the range of institutions, mechanisms, instruments and processes available to manage violent conflict – and in national, regional and international willingness to use force in situations of violent conflict. However, more has not necessarily meant better. In fact, the multiplicity of actors and responses means that the problem of late, incoherent, fragmented, and confused response is perhaps greater today than it was at the time of the Rwandan genocide. If the problem was then that "early warning is not wired to the bulb", today it may be that there are too many bulbs competing with each other and not working when they should.

External response capabilities to situations of violent conflict and state fragility have evolved significantly since the genocide in Rwanda and the Balkan conflicts in the 1990s. As explained in a 2005 ICG review of European Union crisis response capacity, since 2002 "much has changed for the better in both conflict prevention and conflict management. Mechanisms then only planned or just introduced such as the Political and Security Committee are functioning well; important new ones such as the European Defence Agency have come on line. The enlarged EU has gained experience with police and military missions in the Balkans and Africa and has just launched its most ambitious operation, replacing NATO as Bosnia's primary security provider" (ICG, 2005). Similarly, capabilities among regional organisations has grown, with stronger mandates, new protocols, additional committees and departments, and increased staffing seen in the AU, ECOWAS, IGAD, SADC, and ECCAS.

Beyond the growth of institutional capabilities, much has also been learned about the different operational and structural prevention measures that can be used as responses to violent conflict (see Table 3.1 for samples of both types of measures from the Carnegie Commission, and the 2001 *OECD/DAC Guidelines on Conflict Prevention* for more information).

A robust review of capabilities for early and rapid response to violent conflicts and state fragility requires a clear understanding of the institutions involved and the mechanisms, processes and instruments used to deliver responses, as well as the response "toolbox" itself (see Figure 3.1). It also needs to consider good practice and the obstacles to such practice, along with the evidence base for decision making – particularly as they present themselves at the level of implementation. Such a thorough review, however, is not within the scope of this discussion. Rather, in order to draw some preliminary conclusions on early and rapid response, this chapter provides: *(a)* an overview of findings from evaluations of operational and structural prevention; *(b)* drawing from this and other literature, some observations on good practice in response; *(c)* a survey sample of selected response delivery mechanisms/instruments from different agencies that have participated in this report; and *(d)* a discussion of the challenges in the warning-response link in greater detail.

Table 3.1. **Examples of operational and structural prevention**

Operational prevention	Structural prevention
Early warning "A systematic and practical early warning system should be combined with consistently updated contingency plans for preventive action. This would be a radical advance on the present system where, when a trigger event sets off an explosion of violence, it is usually too difficult, too costly, and too late for a rapid and effective response."	*International laws, norms, and agreements* "International laws, norms, agreements, and arrangements — bilateral, regional, and global in scope — are designed to minimise threats to security directly."
Preventive diplomacy "Through bilateral, multilateral, and unofficial channels—to pressure, cajole, arbitrate, mediate, or lend 'good offices' to encourage dialogue and facilitate a non-violent resolution of the crisis."	*Rule of law* "Four essential elements provide a framework for maintaining a just regime for internal stability: a corpus of laws that is legitimately derived and widely promulgated and understood; a consistent, visible, fair, and active network of police authority to enforce the laws (especially important at the local level); an independent, equitable, and accessible grievance redress system, including above all an impartial judicial system; and a penal system that is fair and prudent in meting out punishment."
Economic measures "Sanctions serve three broad policy functions: to signal international concern to the offending state (and, by example, to others), to punish a state's behavior, and to serve as an important precursor to stronger actions." "Inducements involve granting a political or economic benefit in exchange for a specified policy adjustment. [...] Examples of inducements include: favorable trade terms, tariff reductions, direct purchases, subsidies for exports or imports, economic and military aid, favorable taxation, granting access to advanced technology, military co-operation, [etc]."	*Justice* "States should develop ways to promote international law with particular emphasis in three main areas: human rights; humanitarian law, including the need to provide the legal underpinning for UN operations in the field; and non-violent alternatives for dispute resolution, including more flexible intrastate mechanisms for mediation, arbitration, grievance recognition, and social reconciliation."
The use of force "Any threat or use of force must be governed by universally accepted principles, as the UN Charter requires. Decisions to use force must not be arbitrary or operate as the coercive and selectively used weapon of the strong against the weak". "There are three distinct kinds of operations where the use of force and forces — that is, military or police personnel —may have an important role in preventing the outbreak or recurrence of violent conflict: post-conflict peacekeeping, preventive deployments, and 'fire brigade' deployments."	*Sustainable development* "Development efforts to meet [decent living] standards are a prime responsibility of governments, and the international community has a responsibility to help governments through development assistance. Assistance programs are vital to many developing states, crucial to sustaining millions of people in crises, and necessary to help build otherwise unaffordable infrastructure."
	Governance "Transitions to participatory governance, or restoring legitimate governance following conditions of anarchy, may require temporary power sharing. Many forms of power sharing are possible, but all provide for widespread participation in the reconstruction effort, sufficient resources to ensure broad-based access to educational, economic, and political opportunities, and the constructive involvement of outsiders."

Source: Adapted from Chapters 3 and 4 of the Carnegie Commission on Preventing Deadly Conflict (1997), Final Report, New York, December.

PREVENTING VIOLENCE, WAR AND STATE COLLAPSE – ISBN - 978-92-64-05980-1 – © OECD 2009

Figure 3.1. **The institutions, delivery mechanisms, and toolbox of responses to violent conflict**

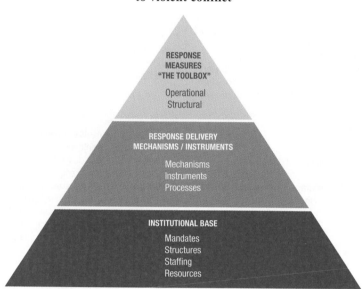

Evaluating responses to violent conflict

Evaluation of responses to violent conflict is a relatively immature if growing field. However, there are numerous evaluations that tell us how difficult responding effectively to violent conflict really is. As explained by Slim (2006) in a review of mediation efforts, "Third-party mediation in international and non-international armed conflict is highly political, fluid and complex. It involves careful long term engagement in situations where widespread human suffering is common and thousands of lives are at stake. Many armed conflicts are deep and protracted with painful histories of extreme violence, inter-group hatred, oppression, humiliation, profound political suspicion and active involvement of other states."

Most evaluations of responses to violent conflict tend to have an institutional, sectoral ("toolbox"-specific) and/or country focus. Useful too is the presence of a range of practice communities that reflect on different elements of operational (*e.g.* Oslo Forum[1] – Improving the Mediation of Armed Conflict) and structural (*e.g.* conflictsensitivity.org[2]) prevention. There are very few publicly available evaluations that deal with *response delivery mechanisms and instruments* – that is, the link between institutions and the measures they implement in response to violent conflict. Among governmental, regional and international organisations, such delivery mechanisms are usually termed "protocols", "instruments", "approaches" or "processes". Here we will look at some of the broader findings on response and try to draw out identified good practice.

Challenges

Numerous challenges are identified in the literature on responding to violent conflicts, and practitioners interviewed in the course of this review also shared their experiences. Some summary observations follow:

- The role of evidence in determining response (as opposed to political expediency, budgetary considerations, etc.) remains limited. Even more linked is the sharing of evidence between organisations – a critical prerequisite for shared problem definition and therefore integrated responses (Fall, 2008).

- *Ad hoc*ism and limited strategic thinking is prevalent. Many actors do not define or share a clear strategy for supporting peace in violent conflict situations. The absence of such strategic frameworks leads to incoherence and uncoordinated responses. It also has efficiency consequences in the implementation of responses (Austin *et al.*, 2004).

- Sustainability concerns remain unaddressed. How can responses be designed to outlast themselves? Whether related to macro-level level strategies for stabilisation or sector-specific approaches (DDR, etc.), how can responses be designed and implemented to ensure sustainability? These questions remain largely unanswered (Sriram and Wermester, 2003).

- Stove piped responses, based on narrow institutional interests and the "hammer seeing every problem as a nail" syndrome, have not been overcome. Deep divisions between security and development agencies, and a propensity for "blueprints" in response to different countries with problems perceived as similar remain important challenges (World Bank, 2006).

Emerging good practice?

Whereas it is difficult and perhaps inadvisable to draw any broad-brush conclusions from very different fields of work, especially given the specific contexts in which they were undertaken, understanding "good" and "bad" practice is critical for any assessment of existing early/rapid response mechanisms. Some important findings in the literature surveyed and interviews include:

- **Understand the problem, establish the ground truth**. Easy access to information and analysis of violent conflict places responders today in a far better position than 15 years ago. However, it also creates a problem of information overload and sometimes leads to paralysis. Nonetheless, there is no way around the complexity of violent conflict, and it is commonsensical that decision making has to be based on an understanding of the issues at stake. Information overload is just part of the burden of dealing with such issues. What is often lost to agencies outside conflict areas (and even some operating out of capitals in affected countries), though, is the "ground truth" (facts or assessments that are confirmed in an actual *field* check). Decisions taken on assessments that are not "ground-truthed" may cost lives or simply feed into mis-/disinformation campaigns by conflicting parties.

- **Ensure that responses are diverse, flexible, adaptable and sustained**. A diverse package of measures is needed to address the multifaceted range of issues in violent conflict contexts. Rapidly changing conflict environments also mean that responses need to be adaptable and flexible. Research shows that following prolonged and vicious violent conflicts, efforts lasting a decade or more are needed to give sustainable peace a real chance. As such, in addition to diversity, flexibility, and adaptation, responses have to be sustained over time (Smith, 2003).

- **Invest time in planning and strategy**. When a response to violent conflict is considered, attention is often given primarily to what is in the institutional toolbox and to existing capacities (what can we do?) rather than what needs to be done to secure an effective outcome (linking capacities to needs). The frequent absence of a comprehensive strategy that defines the goals of a response and identifies steps to reach it means that the resulting approach often remains fragmented. Addressing this strategic and planning deficit is important (Zeeuw, 2001).

- **Be conflict-sensitive**. Over the past decade or so there has been a growing realisation that responses (humanitarian assistance, development aid, political processes, security measures) to violent conflict sometimes feed that conflict rather than alleviate it. This led to the development of different methodologies, including Anderson's "Do No Harm" (1999) and the Peace and Conflict Impact Assessment (PCIA) Resource Pack (2004). Ensuring proper management of the risks and opportunities of knock-on effects (positive and negative) of responses to conflict is important. In practice, being conflict-sensitive refers to the ability of an agency to understand the context, understand the interaction between a response and the context, and act upon this understanding (PCIA Resource Pack, 2004).

- **Do not push technical solutions onto political problems**. Many development agencies (and some peacebuilding NGOs) often approach violent conflict as something that has clear technical solutions. There is a tendency to overlook the politics of technical actions, muddle or cover political actions with technical ones, or (worse) use technical measures as an excuse not to undertake needed political action. Part of this "overlooking", "muddling", and "replacing" is deliberate and flows naturally from engagement in highly sensitive and delicate situations. Although there are issues that require purely technical solutions, blindly pushing such solutions is inadvisable.

- **Be fast, ensure ownership and co-ordination**. Good intentions and generous promises mean little if they are not translated into flexible resources that address the immediate needs of populations affected by conflict. The loss of valuable time from the moment a pledge is given to disbursement and implementation is explained by internal institutional "supply side" factors (*e.g.* cumbersome bureaucratic procedures, etc.) and external "demand side" factors (*e.g.* limited absorption capacity, etc.). Being fast, *i.e.* responding early or rapidly, is critical. However, rapidity is often at the expense of local ownership (necessary for sustainability) and co-ordination (a prerequisite for efficiency and impact) with other agencies. Ways to be fast and bolster ownership and co-ordination, although important, remain elusive (Zeeuw, 2001).

The survey: early and rapid response mechanisms and instruments

Overview

The survey conducted as part of this report looked at response delivery mechanisms and instruments. The basic hypothesis is that institutions will deliver better and faster responses to violent conflict and state fragility if they have pre-established mechanisms/instruments to do so. Respondents were asked a set of questions, for example on the focus, funding, institutional home and delivery time frames of their response delivery mechanisms/instruments (see Box 3.1 for the full set of questions).

Box 3.1. **Survey questions on response delivery mechanisms and instruments**

1. What is the operational and geographical focus of the early/rapid response mechanism(s)/instrument(s)?

2. What is the stated objective of the early/rapid response mechanism(s)/instrument(s)?

3. What is the annual budget for your early/rapid response mechanism(s)/instrument(s) and who provides the funding?

4. Where is the early/rapid response mechanism(s)/instrument(s) located within your agency and what factors (*e.g.* budget, public opinion, etc.) influence decisions on whether or not it is to be deployed?

5. How long does it take from decision to deploy to actual deployment (shortest time frame, longest time frame, and average time frame) of your early/rapid response mechanism(s)/instrument(s)?

6. If your early/rapid response mechanism(s)/instrument(s) involves co-operation, co-ordination activities, or partnership with any other external agencies (governments, multilaterals, NGOs, etc.), which agencies are these and what are the forms of co-operation/co-ordination/partnership?

7. What do you see as the main strengths and limitations/challenges faced by your early response/rapid mechanism(s)/instrument(s)?

8. Are there any success stories or particular impacts that your early/rapid response mechanism(s)/instrument(s) has/have been responsible for?

Many respondents stressed that although they had response mechanisms or instruments, they did not claim that these were necessarily either early or rapid. Another caveat is that the survey was focused on political and developmental actors, not security agencies. Hence, security response instruments (often critically important) are not covered here.[3]

Among OECD DAC members, response mechanisms were present in the State Department of the United States, the Department of Foreign Affairs and International Trade of Canada, the Ministry of Foreign Affairs of the Netherlands and the United Kingdom government. Other governments use more reactive mechanisms or rely on inter-governmental organisations for this task. Indeed, among the inter-governmental agencies surveyed, most had or are developing different response mechanisms and instruments. These include several mechanisms in the United Nations, European Commission, IGAD, ECOWAS, and World Bank. It was not possible to survey NGOs comprehensively. However, among those that run early warning systems, several (FEWER-Eurasia, Foundation for Tolerance International, Foundation for Co-Existence, and WANEP) have very localised response mechanisms. See Table 3.2 for an overview.

Table 3.2. **Governmental, inter-governmental, and non-governmental early/rapid response mechanisms**

Governmental early/rapid response mechanisms	Inter-governmental early/rapid response mechanisms	Non-governmental early/rapid response mechanisms
Department of State (United States): - Conflict Response Fund - Active Response Corps	United Nations: - United Nations Framework Team - UNDP SURGE Mechanism - UNDP Track 113 - UNDP Thematic Trust Fund	FEWER-Eurasia (Russia): - Peace Reconstruction Pool - Humanitarian Dialogue Roundtables - Constructive Direct Action
Department of Foreign Affairs and International Trade (Canada): Stabilisation and Reconstruction Task Force (START) and Global Peace and Security Fund (GPSF)	European Commission: - EU Instrument for Stability	Foundation for Tolerance International (Kyrgyzstan): Non-Violent Conflict Resolution Programme
Netherlands Ministry of Foreign Affairs (Netherlands): Netherlands Stability Fund	IGAD: - CEWARN/CEWERU - Rapid Response Fund (under development)	Foundation for Co-Existence (Sri Lanka): Program for Human Security and Co-existence
UK Government: - Conflict Prevention Pool - Stabilisation Aid Fund - Global Opportunities Fund - Country Offices (contingency planning)	ECOWAS: Mechanism for Conflict Prevention, Conflict Management, Resolution, Peacekeeping and Security	West Africa Network for Peace-Building (Ghana): National WANEP Networks
Federal Department of Foreign Affairs (Switzerland): Swiss Expert Pool	World Bank: - OP8.00 Rapid Response to Crises and Emergencies	

Governmental mechanisms and instruments

Most governmental response mechanisms and instruments are designed to ensure more co-ordinated and coherent responses to crises. They are in the majority of cases funding and expertise instruments used to support a range of political, diplomatic, developmental and security initiatives.

As explained in the Canadian response to the survey, "To enhance the Government of Canada's capacity for international crisis response", the Stabilization and Reconstruction Task Force (START) was established in 2005. START's mission has several components, which include: *(a)* ensuring timely, co-ordinated and effective responses to international crises (natural and human-made) requiring whole-of-government action; *(b)* planning and delivering coherent, effective conflict prevention and crisis response initiatives in states in transition, when Canadian interests are implicated; and *(c)* managing the Global Peace and Security Fund (GPSF), a CAD 142 million financial resource (fiscal year 2006-07), used to develop and deliver peace and security initiatives in such areas as human security, global peace support operations, and global peace and security. START, through the Global Peace and Security Fund (GPSF), supports peace processes and mediation efforts, develops transitional justice and reconciliation initiatives, builds peace enforcement and peace operations capabilities, promotes civilian protection strategies in humanitarian contexts, and reduces the impact of landmines, small arms and light weapons. The GPSF ensures effective, measurable results in support of Canada's priorities in fragile states.

While expertise instruments are normally managed by one government agency, funding mechanisms normally involve a joined-up-government approach. For example, the UK government's Conflict Prevention Pool (originally two pools, one for Africa and one global, and established in 2001) is jointly administered by the Ministry of Defence (MOD), the Department for International Development (DFID), and the Foreign and Commonwealth Office. The Canadian (START) approach involves different levels of co-ordination. The START group:

- Acts as a catalyst or convenor, taking the lead in bringing together all relevant geographic and functional partners in DFAIT and the Canadian government.

- Co-leads crisis management efforts with geographic counterparts, as is the case for most natural disasters and in Haiti and Sudan.

- Provides targeted policy and program support under the leadership of a country-specific DFAIT division, as in the case of Afghanistan.

There are different links between governmental mechanisms/instruments for response and those for warning. In most cases, finance for responses is guided by country and institutional strategies that are informed by some kind of analysis. The use of funding instruments can also be reactive – responding and providing support to the management of unfolding situations (*i.e.* ongoing crises or conflict situations) according to needs identified by various sources (both internal and external to government). Finally, there are connections between the use of mechanisms/instruments and government conflict early warning systems, fragile states' watch lists, and intelligence reports.

The value added of governmental response mechanisms/instruments identified in surveys and reviews of the available literature is threefold:

- A greater ability to co-ordinate joined-up-government approaches to responding to countries in or at risk of crisis.

- A reduction in costs associated with peacekeeping by supporting more effective conflict prevention efforts.

- More rapid, coherent, and informed responses to situations of violent conflict and state fragility.

As mentioned above, most respondents surveyed stressed that their response mechanisms/instruments were not necessarily rapid or early. Indeed, the time frames involved in the use of these mechanisms/instruments for delivery of response (from the point of decision to use the mechanism/instrument to when funding/expertise is provided), were not easily quantifiable. Another challenge is whether these mechanisms/instruments actually deliver on their objectives and value added. As stated in a March 2004 evaluation of the UK government's Conflict Prevention Pools (CPPs), "It has not been possible to come to a definitive judgement as to whether the additional benefits generated by the CPPs as a whole have been worth all or most of the additional money (around £140 million) that has been spent on them since 2001 […]. The progress achieved through the CPP mechanisms is significant enough to justify their continuation" (Austin *et al.*, 2004).[4]

Inter-governmental mechanisms and instruments

There have been significant developments over the past five to eight years in the institutional base, aims, type and range of response measures, instruments and mechanisms available to international and regional organisations. It should also be noted that the purpose of response mechanisms varies depending on the mandate, expertise, membership and geographic scope of the managing organisation. They are used to deliver responses that cover the whole spectrum of operational and structural prevention. The discussion here will focus on a narrow set of mechanisms/instruments as used by a couple of international and regional organisations. It will also concentrate more on the technical (as opposed to political) mechanisms and instruments.

International organisations

The United Nations, World Bank and European Commission are among the numerous international organisations with established mechanisms and instruments used to deliver responses to violent conflict and situations of state fragility. Of interest here, among several mechanisms/instruments available to each institution, is the United Nations Framework Team, the World Bank's OP 8.00 – Rapid Response to Crises and Emergencies, and the European Commission's Instrument for Stability.

The United Nations' Interdepartmental Framework for Coordination of Preventive Action ("Framework Team") is more of a co-ordination mechanism for response than an instrument. It consists of representatives of different UN departments and agencies, as well as representatives of the UN Country Team from the country concerned. The Framework Team is convened when early warning signals are picked up on impending crisis or in ongoing crisis situations to define strategic and coherent (political, diplomatic, economic, developmental and humanitarian) responses.

The World Bank's Operational Policy 8.00 – Rapid Response to Crises and Emergencies formed in March 2007) was designed to address major adverse economic and/or social impacts resulting from an actual or imminent natural or man-made crisis or disaster. It is implemented by different groups in the Bank.[5] It can support one or more of the following objectives: *(a)* rebuilding and restoring physical assets; *(b)* restoring the means of production and economic activities; *(c)* preserving or restoring essential services; *(d)* establishing and/or preserving human, institutional, and/or social capital, including economic reintegration of vulnerable groups; *(e)* facilitating peace building; *(f)* assisting with the crucial initial stages of building capacity for longer-term reconstruction, disaster management, and risk reduction; and *(g)* efforts to mitigate or avert the potential effects of imminent or future emergencies and crises in countries at high risk. OP 8.00 has a global scope and draws together resources from regular IDA-IBRD funding, the Post-Conflict Fund, the LICUS Trust Fund, and the Global Fund for Disaster Reduction and Recovery.

The European Union's[6] Instrument for Stability has been designed to assist in the prevention of conflict, support political stabilisation in post-conflict settings, and help foster recovery following natural disasters. As a financial instrument, it can support "a broad range of initiatives in support of conflict prevention and peacebuilding [...], including confidence-building and mediation efforts, direct support to interim administrations, reform of the security system, support to transitional justice mechanisms, demobilisation and reintegration programming, and strengthening of civil society" (Banim, 2008). Measures funded through the Instrument for Stability need to be aligned with European Commission Country Strategy Papers and National Indicative Programs.

Regional organisations

As mentioned earlier in Chapter 1, regional organisations today have much-enhanced (and growing) capabilities for response (see also European Parliament, 2008). The focus here is placed on the CEWERU mechanism of CEWARN (IGAD) and the ECOWAS Mechanism for Conflict Prevention, Conflict Management, Resolution, Peacekeeping and Security.

The early response component of IGAD's CEWARN is the Conflict Early Warning and Early Response Unit (CEWERU) (see CEWARN's organisation in Figure 3.2). Organised at national level in the countries covered by the Karamoja Cluster (Ethiopia, Kenya, Sudan and Uganda) and Somali Cluster (Ethiopia, Kenya and Somalia), it involves state and non-state representatives at local and national levels. Its purpose is explicitly to respond to CEWARN warnings – and it is to be complemented by Sub-Regional Peace Councils in the near future. The actual *modus operandi* of the CEWERUs is described in Case Study 2 on Pokot in Box 3.2.

Figure 3.2. **Organisational structure of the CEWARN mechanism**

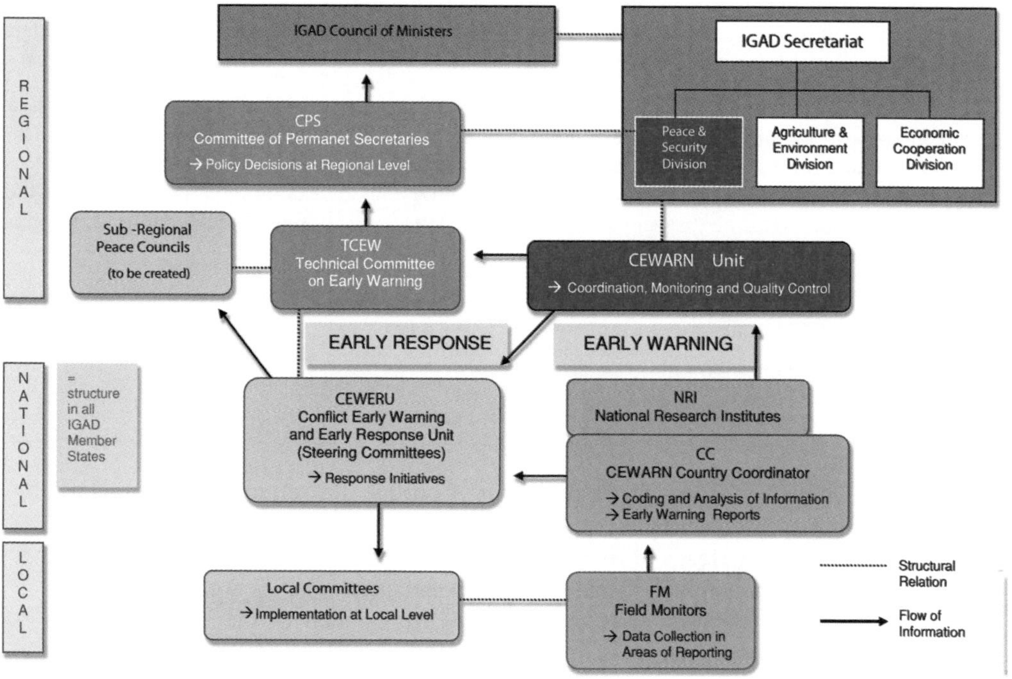

Source: CEWARN Strategy 2007-2011.

Box 3.2. **Case Study 2: An early warning success story from CEWARN in Kenya/Uganda**

On 23 November 2007 the CEWARN Field Monitor for Pokot (Kenya) received an alert from the field that around 100 Pokot warriors were preparing to attack the Bukwo Barracks where their animals were located. The Uganda Peoples Defence Forces (UPDF) in Bukwo had previously recovered these from the Sabiny.

The CEWARN Field Monitor tried to get in touch with the Field Monitor for Bukwo district but failed. He then called on the CEWARN/IGAD Assistant Country Coordinator (ACC) in Uganda. The ACC quickly responded by raising the CEWERU Head at around 23:00, who then got in touch with the UPDF and local authorities in the area. The ACC Uganda alerted the CEWARN/IGAD Country Coordinator and ACC in Kenya about the same. A CEWARN Alert was immediately circulated to the CEWERU Head in Uganda, the CC and the ACC in Kenya.

When notified, the UPDF and Bukwo district local authorities also got in touch with their counterparts on the Kenyan side about the impending attack by the Pokot warriors. The Kenyan authorities quickly passed on information to the Pokot leaders, warning them not to cross the border. They were informed that the UPDF was expecting their attack and that the consequences would be disastrous. The Pokot leaders were advised to be patient as authorities on both sides of the border were trying to resolve the issue peacefully.

The attack by the Pokot warriors from Kenya was successfully prevented – and many lives most likely saved.

Source: Adapted from CEWARN material.

The ECOWAS Mechanism for Conflict Prevention, Management, Resolution, Peacekeeping and Security ("the Mechanism") is a vehicle for the ECOWAS Heads of State to respond preventively to gross human rights violations, situations of mass violence and genocide, as well as political crisis and instability. It is also operated by Council of the Wise, and the Mediation and Security Council. It helps ECOWAS deliver a range of political, diplomatic, and security responses to crises in the West African sub-region, as well as in Africa as a whole, through the availability of the Stand-By Force for AU missions. Funded mainly by ECOWAS, USAID, Africa Peace Facility (African Union) and the African Development Bank (ADB), interventions in Liberia, Guinea Bissau, Togo and Guinea are cited as success stories in the use of the Mechanism. ECOWAS also runs ECOWARN, and in theory the Mechanism should draw on early warnings to catalyse response. However, according to interviews, this potential remains to be fully exploited.

The value added of inter-governmental (international and regional) response mechanisms/instruments identified in surveys and through interviews is threefold:

- They provide agreed upon mechanisms for the delivery of a variety of responses (financial, political, diplomatic, developmental, security) to crises, and may enable rapid (and in some cases early) responses.

- They promote more trust building and consensus-based decision making both within the bureaucracy of an inter-governmental organisation and (more importantly) among member governments to a crisis situation.

- They serve as a resource to help avoid the derailment of developmental investments by crises and conflicts.

The main challenges associated with inter-governmental response mechanisms/instruments, of course, are related to the inter-governmental nature of these institutions and the associated obstacles to response. These obstacles include a lack of political will and sensitivities about state sovereignty. There are also important bureaucratic and institutional challenges with cumbersome procedures that undermine the rapid and early delivery of responses. Interviewees have moreover stressed the limited link between warning and response in inter-governmental bodies. The weakness in this link relates not only to bureaucratic obstacles, but also to the lack of incentive mechanisms and weak sensitisation of political decision makers on the value of early warning and evidence-based decision making.

Non-governmental mechanisms and instruments

Non-governmental crisis response mechanisms and instruments exist at the micro level, although regional NGO networks involved in prevention (like WANEP) and global ones (like GPAC) may have advocacy mechanisms (statements of concern, media campaigns, etc.) that are designed to promote responses among larger actors. It is not the purpose of this report to chart these networks or their response mechanisms/instruments. Rather, a brief overview of response mechanisms and instruments at the micro level and among NGOs that run early warning systems is given.

Two types of NGO/community response mechanisms will be described here: *(a)* response planning roundtables; and *(b)* field-level direct responses to violence.

As mentioned in Chapter 1, in 2001 FEWER, WANEP, the EastWest Institute, and the OSCE Conflict Prevention Centre launched a roundtable process that brought state and non-state (local, national and international) decision makers together to formulate joint strategies for response to early warnings. The purpose was to address incoherence in responses by different actors through joint problem definition and planning, as well as to provide a forum for multi-stakeholder discussion on early warnings as and when they emerged. The roundtable process was piloted first in Javakheti (Georgia) and Guinea-Conakry. Later, it extended to the North Caucasus, became part of the FAST agenda, and was further developed as a concept by other agencies and groups.

Most conflict prevention NGOs and civil society organisations active in countries affected by crisis and conflict are involved in responding to situations of impending or actual violence. This work has been documented extensively in case studies by groups such as CDA Inc.[7] Standardised response mechanisms are relatively new but are now often present in NGOs that run early warning systems. These mechanisms will link monitoring of crisis situations to responses (fact-finding, mediation, dialogue) through a set of standard operating procedures. Such procedures for response are often found in "third generation" early warning initiatives as well as in corporate early warning systems (see Case Study 3 on the Eastern Province in Sri Lanka in Box 3.3).

Box 3.3. **Case Study 3: An early response from the Foundation for Co-Existence in the Eastern Province**

On 18 June 2005, communal clashes broke out between Tamils and Sinhalese in the township of Seruvila in the Trincomalee district of the Eastern Province. These followed the killing by unidentified gunmen of a Sinhalese police sergeant who was a resident in the area. Seruvila is a Sinhalese township and its geography is such that road access to the nearby Tamil villages leads through it. Rumours that the police sergeant was assassinated by Tamil militants led to serious restiveness among Sinhalese youth in Seruvila. They assaulted of a group of Tamil civilians who were travelling on the road, damaged vehicles and blocked supplies to the Tamil villages. In retaliation the Tamil youths unleashed violence against the Sinhalese in the border area, using hand grenades. FCE's information centre was monitoring the situation on a daily basis and foresaw the escalation of deadly ethnic violence. The information centre co-ordinated with the early response unit and dispatched two missions of field monitors to discuss the issues with the Sinhalese community leaders and the LTTE local political leadership. Following these discussions, the FCE was able to bring the parties to negotiations where they agreed to stop hostilities and resolve the issues peacefully.

Source: Adapted from FCE material.

The value added of the non-governmental/community response mechanisms and instruments described here is twofold:

- They facilitate joint problem definition and response planning among a diverse group of agencies to early warnings.

- They help deliver quick responses to micro-level crisis situations that may deteriorate into violence and lead to the loss of lives.

The challenges of non-governmental response mechanisms/instruments are significant. They relate to the small size of the organisations (and limits to convening power, types of measures, etc.), vulnerability to interference or intimidation by state or non-state actors, and often the inability of NGOs/civil society organisations to work together for political/personal reasons. One interviewee expressed disappointment, for example, that civil society networks in Kenya had been unable to respond effectively to the post-election violence that affected that country in early 2008.

Preliminary conclusions – more does not mean better

There are a range of early and rapid response mechanisms/instruments among governments, multilaterals, and NGOs. These mechanisms and instruments play an important role in facilitating potentially effective, early, and rapid responses to violent conflict. However, although capacities have increased over the last decade, more capacity does not necessarily mean better responses. Among the key preliminary conclusions are these:

- The links between different early/rapid response mechanisms/instruments and a sound, field-based understanding of the issues vary significantly. In many cases, decisions regarding if and how to deploy a mechanism/instrument are not driven by an analysis of what is needed and what works but by other concerns. However, among regional organisations and NGOs that run early warning systems, the use of evidence-based decision making (caveat: when analyses are sound) seems more widespread.

- Many funding- and expertise-based mechanisms/instruments have a relatively short time span and are mostly one-offs. They are also frequently "demand driven", *i.e.* used to fund specific requests for assistance or proposals received. There are some cases (*e.g.* the UK Conflict Prevention Pool) where the use of instruments falls within a preventive strategy for a given conflict.

- It is unclear how "early" and "rapid" governmental and inter-governmental response mechanisms/instruments are. The NGOs surveyed, in part due to their small and highly focused response mechanisms/instruments, were able to give concrete estimates on deployment time scales. Among agencies (governmental and inter-governmental) with larger and more sophisticated response mechanisms/instruments, there was frequently no answer on time scales. Whereas many mechanisms/instruments involve in-house (joined-up-government or inter-agency) co-ordination, there is little evidence to suggest that the deployment of mechanisms/instruments is co-ordinated among different governments, multilateral agencies and NGOs.

The warning-response link

It is well-accepted that early warning without an early or rapid response is pointless. An early or rapid response that is ineffective, *i.e.* that does not contribute to the management, resolution, or prevention of violent conflict (or state failure/collapse), is also futile or worse. The past decade has seen important developments in the capability of international and regional institutions to respond. However, there is a significant list of post-Rwanda crises, most recently in Kenya and Chad, where early and rapid response has been lacking and where thousands of lives have been lost. Frequently, the absence of response is blamed on "a lack of political will". The sections above have flagged two elements of this "political will" deficit: weak early warning, and limits to current international and regional response mechanisms/instruments (see Figure 3.3). A third element, discussed here, is a set of personal, institutional, and political shortcomings (Table 3.3).

Figure 3.3. **Unpacking the lack of political will**

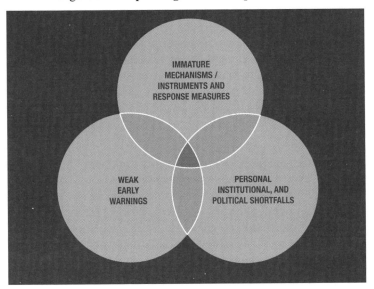

Table 3.3. **Personal, institutional, and political factors that affect response**

Personal	Institutional	Political
• Time and decision-making pressure • Competing priorities • Personal interest and experience • Knowledge and understanding of situation • Training and analytical skills • Decision-making ability • Risk taking profile • Personal relationships • Personal cost-benefit calculations and accountability • Available information and analysis	• Institutional and departmental mandate • Budget availability • Turf considerations • Risk taking/averse culture • Personnel turnover and institutional memory • Decision-making procedures • Available mechanisms and instruments • Accountability considerations • Security of staff	• National/institutional interest and priorities • Alliances and special relationships • Enmities and competition • Party and constituency politics • Media coverage and CNN effects • Advocacy pressure • Political cost-benefit calculations • Political consensus • Politicisation of information

Source: Drawn from Steering Committee of the Joint Evaluation of Emergency Assistance to Rwanda (1996), *The International Response to Conflict and Genocide: Lessons from the Rwanda Experience,* March; Carment, D., Y. Samy and S. Prest (2007), "Determinants of State Fragility and Implications for Aid Allocation: An Assessment", CIFP, Carleton University, Ottawa, May; Matveeva, A. (2006), *Early Warning and Early Response: Conceptual and Empirical Dilemmas,* GPAC Issue Paper No. 1, September; and Nyheim, D. (2003), "What Can Be Done?" in Carol Rittner, John K. Roth and James M. Smith (eds.), *Will Genocide Ever End?*, Paragon House.

Decision making on how to respond to situations of violent conflict and state fragility is driven in part by personal, institutional and political factors. It is personal, as individual experience, personal relationships, etc. profoundly affect the decisions on response. It is institutional, as *e.g.* turf battles, personnel turnover and budget disbursement procedures also determine what choices are made. And it is political: national interests, the work of advocacy and interest groups, and special relationships, *inter alia*, have real implications for choices on how to respond to violent conflict and state fragility.

It is important to understand the personal, institutional and political factors that affect responses to violent conflict and state fragility. Such an understanding serves not only to contextualise the role of early warning and response capabilities, but also to identify the basic issues that need to be tackled in efforts to bridge the gap between warning and response. Table 3.3 summarises the most salient of these at a governmental and inter-governmental level (although they are also applicable to NGO decision makers) as identified in the literature and through interviews.

Table 3.3 has a number of implications:

- There are many personal, institutional, and political considerations that affect decision makers and lead to a focus on what *cannot* be done, or (at best) what *can* be done, as opposed to what *should* be done about violent conflict or fragile states. Context requirements are overshadowed by other influences.

- Institutional culture and capacity play a determining role in whether appropriate decisions are taken and responses follow. Many institutions deter or punish individual risk taking, apply restrictive interpretations on their mandates, have cumbersome and hierarchical decision-making processes, and lack operational response mechanisms and instruments.

- There remains a significant accountability deficit for inaction or poor action in responding to violent conflict and state failure. Whereas some multinational companies have been known to fire employees if inadequate preventive measures have led to the loss of corporate assets, few (if any) civil servants lose their jobs when decades of development investments are destroyed by violent conflict.

Together these factors complicate efforts to respond to conflict and state fragility. Additional complications come from the rapid internationalisation of many crises linked to contemporary threat perceptions. There is today far greater international political interest in conflicts that were previously considered marginal (*e.g.* Beluchistan, Somalia, and Northern Ghana). Because of additional agendas, actors and engagement, this internationalisation (with some exceptions, of course) often complicates efforts to respond to conflict and state fragility quickly and effectively.

Analytical conclusions

It is clear that capabilities to respond to situations of violent conflict and state fragility have evolved significantly since the genocide in Rwanda and the Balkan conflicts in the 1990s. Institutional mandates and response mechanisms have been strengthened, funding has increased, there is a greater range of operational tools, and mechanisms have been refined on the basis of experience.

From evaluations of responses to violent conflict, several "good practice" principles have been drawn by scholars, including: *(a)* understand the problem, hold the "ground truth"; *(b)* ensure that responses are diverse, flexible, adaptable and sustainable; *(c)* invest time in planning and strategy; *(d)* be conflict-sensitive; *(e)* do not push technical solutions onto political problems; *(f)* balance speed, ownership and co-ordination.

The review identified numerous important gains from the development of governmental, inter-governmental and non-governmental response mechanisms/instruments:

- More rapid, coherent, and informed responses within institutions to situations of violent conflict and state fragility.

- Perceived potential for reduced costs associated with expensive "late" responses to violent conflict and state fragility.

- The promotion of more consensus-based decision making within both the bureaucracies and political leadership to a crisis situation; and

- A resource to help avoid the derailment of developmental investments by crises and conflict.

However, more mechanisms/instruments have not translated into better responses. The link between warning and response remains weak. This is due to the poor quality of early warning and immature mechanisms/instruments and response measures, along with a range of personal, institutional, and political shortcomings affecting decision making. If the problem was that "early warning is not wired to the bulb", today there are too many bulbs competing with each other or not working when they should.

PREVENTING VIOLENCE, WAR AND STATE COLLAPSE – ISBN - 978-92-64-05980-1 – © OECD 2009

Notes

1. See *www.osloforum.org*.

2. See *www.conflictsensitivity.org*.

3. See the *Compendium of Surveyed Early Warning Systems and Early Response Mechanisms/Instruments* in the annex for profiles of systems covered.

4. It is important to stress here that much has probably changed with the CPP mechanisms since the evaluation was undertaken – these changes remain outside of the scope of this report.

5. On conflict-related crises and emergencies, OP 8.00 is managed by the Fragile and Conflict-Affected Countries Group, Operations Policy and Country Services (OPCS). On natural disaster-related emergencies, it is the Hazard Management Unit, Social Development Network (SDN) that takes co-ordination responsibility.

6. As explained by Banim (2008), with the mainstreaming of conflict and state fragility within different EU instruments, "the entire EUR 6.2 billion (2007 budget forecast) allocated within the Community budget for external actions should be considered in terms of its conflict-prevention potential. Specifically, within this EUR 6.2 billion, EUR 232 million is allocated to the stability instrument and EUR 150 million to the CFSP budget. Separately, EUR 22.7 billion for the period 2008–13 is available within the 10th European Development Fund (EDF) for the 78 African, Caribbean, and Pacific states (ACP). EDF funding typically constitutes 40–70% of ACP national budgets."

7. See, for example, "Confronting War: Critical Lessons For Peace Practitioners" (2003) at *www.cdainc.com/cdawww/pdf/book/ confrontingwar_Pdf1.pdf.*

Chapter 4

Future Directions for Early Warning and Early Response

International threat perceptions have changed since the terrorist attacks on the United States in September 2001. Another mutation in threats is likely over the next decade – involving a mix of repercussions of climate change (water and land scarcity, population displacements), fallout from the wars in Iraq/Afghanistan and the war on terrorism, and the transformation of violent conflict into criminalised armed violence, to mention just a few factors. Whether advances in technology, early warning and global response capabilities are likely to place us in a position to effectively manage these threats is questionable.

The future of conflict early warning and response is likely to be driven by a combination of future security threats, advances in technology and, of course, current warning and response trends. What does that add up to? What are the implications for current early warning and response systems? This chapter attempts to provide some answers to these questions.

Future threats to international security

Future threats to international security are likely to be a mix of existing threats, their mutations or fallout, and emerging as well as unforeseen threats. It is possible to make some observations about the first two, but not the last. The threats of particular concern to the conflict early warning field relate to climate change, fallout from the war in Iraq/Afghanistan and the war on terrorism, and the rise of criminalised armed violence.

Climate-related threats – There is an increasing body of literature on how climate change is likely to affect the future of international security. The magnitude of impact depends on what scientific projections one subscribes to. A relatively balanced view is elaborated in the March 2008 High Representative and European Commission report to the European Council, which observed that "Climate change is best viewed as a threat multiplier which exacerbates existing trends, tensions and instability. The core challenge is that climate change threatens to overburden states and regions which are already fragile and conflict prone. It is important to recognise that the risks are not just of a humanitarian nature; they also include political and security risks that directly affect European interests". The main climate-related threats identified in the report include: *(a)* conflict over resources; *(b)* economic damage and risk to coastal cities and critical infrastructure; *(c)* loss of territory and border disputes; *(d)* environmentally induced migration; *(e)* situations of fragility and radicalisation; *(f)* tension over energy supply; and *(g)* pressure on international governance. Excerpts from the report are given in Box 4.1.

Fallout from the wars in Afghanistan and Iraq – Writing about the wars in Afghanistan and Iraq is politically sensitive and difficult as analyses are polarised between those who believe these wars were justified, and those who think they were unlawful or have been poorly managed. Most, however, agree that the human and financial toll of these wars is or will be significant both in the short and long term (Teslik, 2008). With regard to fallout, or "blow-back", there is much speculation and also polarised disagreement. Indeed, the nature and level of fallout from these wars is likely to be determined by the policies pursued by the next US government. For better or worse – in terms of the global economy, energy supplies, the "war on terror", credibility of Western democracies, the integrity of international laws and norms and inter-faith relations – the wars in Afghanistan and Iraq will have an impact and influence on future security threat scenarios well beyond the actual theatres of operations.

Box 4.1. **Climate-related threats to international security – High Representative and European Commission Report to the European Council, March 2008**

i) Conflict over resources

"Reduction of arable land, widespread shortage of water, diminishing food and fish stocks, increased flooding and prolonged droughts are already happening in many parts of the world. Climate change will alter rainfall patterns and further reduce available freshwater by as much as 20 to 30% in certain regions. A drop in agricultural productivity will lead to, or worsen, food-insecurity in least developed countries and an unsustainable increase in food prices across the board."

ii) Economic damage and risk to coastal cities and critical infrastructure

"It has been estimated that a business as usual scenario in dealing with climate change could cost the world economy up to 20% of global GDP per year, whereas the cost of effective concerted action can be limited to 1%. Coastal zones are the home of about one fifth of the world's population, a number set to rise in the years ahead. Mega-cities, with their supporting infrastructure, such as port facilities and oil refineries, are often located by the sea or in river deltas. Sea-level rise and the increase in the frequency and intensity of natural disasters pose a serious threat to these regions and their economic prospects."

iii) Loss of territory and border disputes

"Scientists project major changes to the landmass during this century. Receding coastlines and submergence of large areas could result in loss of territory, including entire countries such as small island states. More disputes over land and maritime borders and other territorial rights are likely."

iv) Environmentally induced migration

"Those parts of the populations that already suffer from poor health conditions, unemployment or social exclusion are rendered more vulnerable to the effects of climate change, which could amplify or trigger migration within and between countries. The UN predicts that there will be millions of 'environmental' migrants by 2020 with climate change as one of the major drivers of this phenomenon."

Box 4.1. **Climate-related threats to international security – High Representative and European Commission Report to the European Council, March 2008**
(continued)

v) **Situations of fragility and radicalisation**

"Climate change may significantly increase instability in weak or failing states by over-stretching the already limited capacity of governments to respond effectively to the challenges they face. The inability of a government to meet the needs of its population as a whole or to provide protection in the face of climate change-induced hardship could trigger frustration, lead to tensions between different ethnic and religious groups within countries and to political radicalisation. This could destabilise countries and even entire regions."

vi) **Tension over energy supply**

"One of the most significant potential conflicts over resources arises from intensified competition over access to, and control over, energy resources. That in itself is, and will continue to be, a cause of instability. However, because much of the world's hydrocarbon reserves are in regions vulnerable to the impacts of climate change and because many oil and gas producing states already face significant social economic and demographic challenges, instability is likely to increase. This has the potential to feed back into greater energy insecurity and greater competition for resources."

vii) **Pressure on international governance**

"The multilateral system is at risk if the international community fails to address the threats outlined above. Climate change impacts will fuel the politics of resentment between those most responsible for climate change and those most affected by it. Impacts of climate mitigation policies (or policy failures) will thus drive political tension nationally and internationally."

Source: High Representative and European Commission Report to the European Council, March 2008.

The war on terrorism – The fallout from the war on terrorism, also a politically sensitive topic, follows partly from the diversion of political attention and resources away from important global challenges, as well as from compromises made in different parts of the world on accountability and governance. Global challenges include not only those mentioned above and below, but also current and future worldwide financial instability and energy scarcity. Compromises made on accountability of government and governance has meant that groups and regimes responsible for human rights abuses and crimes are given legitimacy and support (*e.g.* Afghanistan, Ethiopia in Somalia, etc.) (Human Rights Watch, 2008). Knock-on effects of diverted attention/resources and compromised governance are difficult to anticipate, but will be felt regionally and globally.

The rise of criminalised armed violence – In many violent conflict situations, grievance is increasingly overshadowed by greed, and violence is becoming an end in itself. Somalia, the Niger Delta, Colombia, Haiti and Chechnya, as well as Iraq and Afghanistan, are all examples of this trend. Approaching such violent conflicts (or situations of armed violence) from a traditional operational and structural prevention angle is probably inappropriate. Engaging with non-state actors that either have no political agendas or use politics as a fig leaf for criminal intent is very different from engagement with groups motivated by grievance. However, in situations where greed dominates, grievance often remains. As more violent conflicts mutate into situations of armed violence, early warning and response approaches must also adapt to facilitate the search for sustainable solutions.

Advances in technology

Emerging trends in conflict early warning can also be seen in the use of new technologies. Google Earth, Geographical Information Systems or GIS (see Figure 4.1 on Afghanistan), and search engines are used more frequently.

Increased communication capacities, particularly with the now widespread use of mobile phones, help to enhance connections between warners and responders – but only where such links are either informally agreed or formally established (see for example Case Study 2 in Box 3.2).

Advances in global navigation satellite systems (GPS, or the European Galileo), combined with those in communication technology, are likely to contribute to improved speed and accuracy in pinpointing the location and nature of violent events in crisis-affected countries. They will be of particular importance for early warning systems that operate local information networks and response mechanisms, provided that such systems are able to access the technology.

The Harvard Humanitarian Initiative's (HHI) study entitled "The Untapped Potential of Information Communication Technologies for Conflict Early Warning", completed in August 2008, is a comprehensive and in-depth review of technological advances relevant for the field of conflict early warning (Leaning and Meier, 2008).

Figure 4.1. **Risk map of conflictive events in Afghanistan**

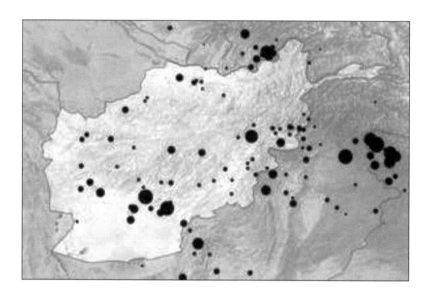

Note: The map displays places of violence encounters.

Source: swisspeace (2007), "FAST Update Afghanistan No. 4", August to September 2007.

The Ushahidi initiative was set up shortly after the Kenyan elections to map and document information on violent events and human rights abuses. Ushahidi draws on crowd sourcing for the collection of crisis information.

The platform takes a decentralised, open source approach to information collection by using Web 2.0 applications, mobile phones and SMS. HHI is also pioneering the field of Crisis Mapping Analytics, or CMA, which draws on advances in statistics and technology to identify and analyse crisis patterns over space and time (see Figure 4.2).

Current trends in warning and response initiatives

Early warning trends

Three trends in the early warning field can immediately be discerned from the above analysis.

- The future of early warning systems is likely to be driven by regional organisations and NGOs based in conflict-affected regions. However, some northern-based initiatives (*e.g.* ICG) will continue to serve as important analytical sources for governments and multilaterals, particularly now that both FEWER and FAST have closed down. Whether it is in the interest of governments and multilaterals to rely heavily on just a few global sources is an important question.

Figure 4.2. **Screenshot from the website of the Ushahidi initiative**

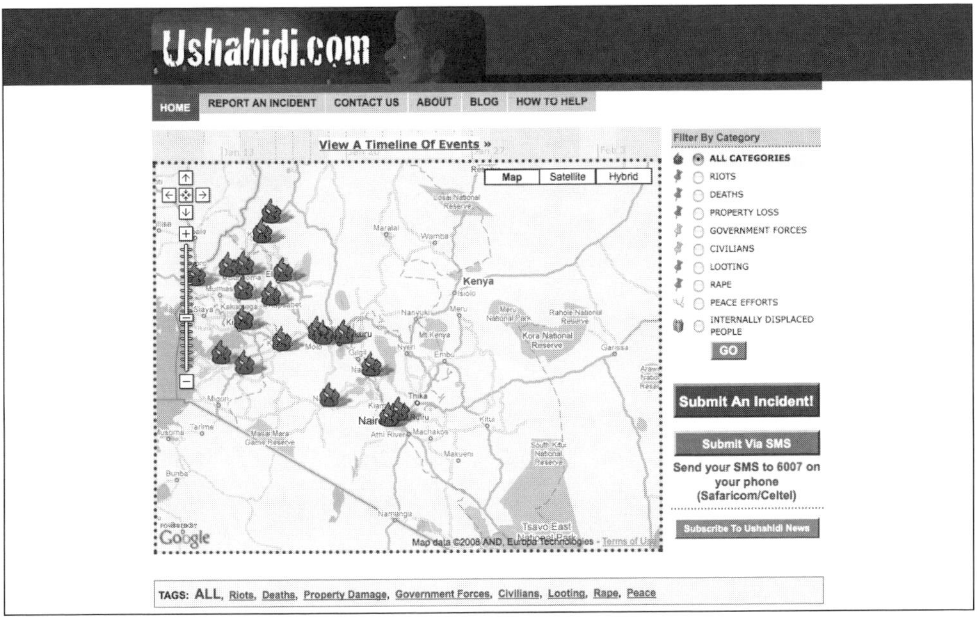

Source: Illustration in Learning and Meier (2008b), drawn from the Ushahidi initiative, *www.ushahidi.com*.

- Development agencies rely more heavily on one-off analyses (conflict and state fragility assessments) to inform programmes than on early warning. This trend is likely to continue and develop, particularly in the direction of assessments of state fragility.

- Another important trend, which has not been discussed in detail due to commercial confidentiality issues, is the increased use of early warning systems by businesses that operate in conflict-affected areas. These systems mirror the third generation ones discussed above and operate at the micro level, particularly around critical assets and investments. They serve to inform joint actions by community leaders, corporate officials and government, as well as corporate social responsibility efforts. Early warning systems and risk assessment tools are important additions to security measures for these companies. Figure 4.3, illustrating a typical corporate conflict risk assessment tool (names and locations changed), is provided courtesy of INCAS Consulting Ltd.

Figure 4.3. **Corporate conflict risk assessment tool**

Source: INCAS Consulting Ltd.

Early response trends

In the field of early and rapid response, there are a few noteworthy trends.

- Joined-up-government approaches and inter-agency co-operation is gaining ground, driven now by OECD/DAC work on whole-of-government approaches (see Box 4.2 on main findings from OECD/DAC thematic meetings on these approaches). If coupled with further development of early response mechanisms and instruments, this may bode well for international and regional efforts to respond early and rapidly to violent conflicts and situations of acute state fragility.

- Decision makers deployed to respond to violent conflicts are still under-trained, over-stretched, rotated too frequently, struggling with cumbersome decision-making processes, and too unaccountable. The situation is unlikely to change and will continue to frustrate those who hope for effective responses to violent conflict and state fragility.

- Along with the increase in response capabilities (institutions, mechanisms/instruments and measures), there is now a greater body of knowledge and experience available on the use of these capabilities in situations of violent conflict and state fragility. Much of this knowledge remains within institutions, but there are ongoing efforts by groups such as the OECD DAC to harness good practice. Scaled-up lesson reviews at the international and regional levels may be an important contribution to bolstering the cause of early/rapid response.

- The emergence of third generation early warning and early response systems, with their potential for more effective regional and micro-level preventive efforts, is promising. Greater investments in such systems may yield important results, particularly in terms of lives and property saved.

Box 4.2. **Main findings of OECD DAC thematic meetings on whole-of-government approaches**

A series of common strategic issues have emerged from OECD DAC thematic meetings that warrant further whole-of government attention. These include:

- How to develop common objectives for diplomatic, defence, security, finance and development actions. Joint analysis and the more systematic use of joint planning tools such as transitional result frameworks (including a set of stabilisation, state-building and peacebuilding goals) are likely to facilitate this process.

- How to provide incentives for officials from different policy communities to work together in capitals and at the field level.

- How OECD governments can support a *whole-of-system* approach, incorporating the efforts of non-OECD governments and international organisations.

- How to manage issues at the frontier between ODA and non-ODA resources and civilian-military collaboration, to maximise development impact.

Source: Adapted from OECD (2008), *Thematic Meetings on Whole-of-Government Approaches to Situations of Conflict and Fragility*, OECD, Paris, May.

Analytical conclusions

Early warning and early response will be faced with an evolution of threats over the next decade. These threats will come from the combined impacts on conflict and instability of climate change, fallout from the wars in Afghanistan/Iraq, the war on terror, and the increasing criminalisation of conflict, among other factors. There is little indication of forward thinking, particularly following the demise of global early warning systems such as FAST and FEWER, among early warners of these issues. However, the future relevance of the field depends largely on work undertaken now to be able to understand and provide useful analysis on these emerging threats.

Technological advancements have played an important role in improving the efficiency and effectiveness of early warning systems. Most inter-governmental and non-governmental systems, however, have not gone beyond the use of email and websites for dissemination and communication technology for data collection. Governmental and some inter-governmental systems do benefit from access to and resources for satellite and GIS in their analysis and reporting. However, access to technology remains very unequal between systems. In general, the field of conflict early warning continues to lag far behind in adopting new technologies and Web 2.0 applications.

There are several important trends in the early warning community that are important to note. First, with the closure of FAST (and previously FEWER), there is now less open source diversity in early warning analysis at a global level. Exclusive reliance on a few sources, no matter how good they are, is not good decision-making practice, particularly on complex issues such as violent conflict and state fragility. Second, development agencies are no longer as enthusiastic about early warning systems as they used to be. Agencies involved in operational prevention remain interested, however, and current early warning systems need to consider how to shift their networking efforts to these actors if they have not done so already. Third, with increased corporate use of early warning and risk assessment tools, there are new partners to bring into the early warning fold.

In terms of early response trends, the following conclusions can be drawn. First, along with work to ensure greater government and inter-governmental coherence, there is a need to empower officials working on conflict and state fragility (through capacity building, etc.) to do their work well. Second, an increase in response capabilities and experience needs to be bolstered by initiatives to document and share good practice. Not doing so will constitute a missed opportunity. And third, micro-level responses to violent conflict by third generation early warning systems are an exciting development in the field that should be encouraged further. These kinds of responses save lives.

Considering the balance between future security threats and trends in technology, early warning and early response, this report concludes that the early warning and response field is unprepared for what is to come – and risks losing its relevance.

Chapter 5

Conclusions and Recommendations

This report has reviewed the history of the early warning field, discussed the range of current early warning tools and operational systems, assessed a selection of early/rapid response mechanisms/instruments, and discussed future directions for the field. What then is the big picture? What does it mean in relation to the critical questions raised in this report? Where is future work required? And what should the OECD DAC and its members do about it? This concluding chapter attempts to answer those questions.

What does it add up to?

Conflict early warning has evolved significantly since its initial conceptualisation, with important contributions from many individuals and organisations over the years. However, can we say today that we are in a position to prevent another Rwandan genocide? We probably cannot. Conflict early warning faces the same challenges as it did 15 years ago. Early response remains elusive, and with it our ability to protect and preserve life in the face of war remains weak.

The conflict early warning field is trying to find a balance between staying relevant to its funders and doing what it is supposed to do. However, it is tilting significantly towards the former, in part because of changes in the geo-strategic environment and Northern perceptions of threats. The notion of an open source, pro-people and pro-peace conflict early warning system is giving way to one with a far more pronounced intelligence dimension.

Advances over the past 15 years or so in early and rapid response have been made in the range of institutions, mechanisms, instruments and measures available to manage violent conflict as well as in national, regional, and international willingness to use force in situations of violent conflict. However, more has not necessarily meant better. In fact, the multiplicity of actors and responses means that the problems of late, incoherent, fragmented and confused responses is perhaps greater today than it was at the time of the Rwandan genocide.

Further transformation of the geo-strategic context and perception of threats is certain to occur over the next decade. This is likely to involve a mix of the repercussions of climate change, fallout from the wars in Iraq and Afghanistan, the war on terror, and the transformation of violent conflict into criminalised armed violence, among other factors. Whether advances in technology, early warning and global response capabilities are likely to place us in a position to effectively manage these threats is questionable.

The big picture that emerges from this report is that 14 years after the Rwandan genocide, early warning systems still cannot claim to be in a position to prevent situations of mass violence. Part of the reason for this is poor early warning. Another part is that efforts to "wire warning to response" have found growing but still immature and incoherent response capabilities along with a set of personal, institutional, and political obstacles to response. As such, the international and regional response mechanisms are working rather poorly. With a future filled will new and significant threats, the early warning and response field needs leadership and a vision to guide its development over the next decade.

Revisiting critical questions

What is the value of early warning for the prevention of violent conflict and peacebuilding? What role does early warning play in prevention?

The review of governmental, inter-governmental, and non-governmental early warning systems concludes that these systems provide:

- A crisis prediction capacity that enables proactive decision making.

- A stronger basis for evidence-based decision making on countries affected by crisis.

- Improved programming through systematic country reviews and expert analysis.

- A priority-setting contribution through watch list-type products.

- A starting point for developing a shared problem definition on crisis-affected countries that sets the stage for more coherent responses.

- An ideas pool for responses, and sometimes the forum to meet fellow responders and plan joint response strategies.

What are the most effective early warning systems? Why they are effective and what impacts do they have?

Governmental, inter-governmental, and non-governmental early warning systems have different purposes. However, it is generally accepted that an effective early warning system: *(a)* is based "close to the ground" or has strong field-based networks of monitors; *(b)* uses multiple sources of information and both qualitative/quantitative analytical methods; *(c)* capitalises on appropriate communication and information technology; *(d)* provides regular reports and updates on conflict dynamics to key national and international stakeholders; and *(e)* has a strong link to responders or response mechanisms.

There are several reported impacts of different systems – including crises averted, lives saved, and informed responses – many of which have been included in this report as case studies. However, more rigorous evaluations of these impacts are required.

What are the strengths and weaknesses of different methodologies – quantitative/qualitative and conflict analysis/state fragility?

Most analytical methods will serve particular institutional interests and agendas – there is, therefore, not necessarily one method that is better than another. The strengths and weaknesses of the quantitative and qualitative methods surveyed are summarised in Table 5.1.

Table 5.1. **Strengths and weaknesses of quantitative and qualitative methods**

	Quantitative methods	Qualitative methods
Strengths	Their predictive capacity, particularly related to political crisis and instability, is high. Their immediate policy value – in terms of priority setting and "watch listing" – is significant. Models that draw on a larger number of significant indicators provide pointers for programming.	They provide rich contextual information and analysis that can be simple enough for desk officers to absorb and incorporate into action. They often have strong planning and evaluation applications built in.
Weaknesses	Unreliable and incomplete data from crisis-affected countries affect reliability of findings. Even the best quantitative models will at times have reduced predictability. The graphs, charts, country lists, etc. in themselves provide little insight to decision makers into what is happening on the ground or what needs to be done.	Unreliable and incomplete data from crisis-affected countries affect reliability of findings. They are often one-off snapshots of rapidly evolving situations and thus quickly outdated. Sometimes they oversimplify the complexity of violent conflict and state fragility situations. Usually they proffer technical solutions to complex political issues. They are fundamentally based on personal judgement.

What does it take to really prevent violent conflict? What do we currently know is good practice that works?

From evaluations of responses to violent conflict, several "good practice" principles have been drawn by scholars, including: *(a)* understand the problem, hold the "ground truth"; *(b)* ensure that responses are diverse, flexible, and sustainable; *(c)* invest time in planning and strategy; *(d)* be conflict-sensitive; *(e)* do not push technical solutions onto political problems; *(f)* balance speed, ownership and co-ordination.

What early/rapid response mechanisms/instruments are available?

There is a range of response mechanisms/instruments hosted by different institutions. However, these response "delivery systems" cannot be dissociated from their host institutions (with the latter's mandates, structures, resources, etc.), or from the operational and structural prevention measures they deliver.

What influences and blocks early response? What are the personal, institutional and political factors at play?

The lack of political will is often cited as the main blocker of early response. This report has sought to unpack "the lack of political will" and argues that it follows from weak warnings, immature response mechanisms/instruments and measures, along with a range of personal, institutional, and political shortfalls. Together, these prevent us from responding in a timely and appropriate manner to situations of violent conflict and state fragility.

Emerging questions and research needs

A set of emerging questions and research needs related to early warning and early response emerge from the chapters above. They include:

- What are the success stories in conflict early warning? Why were these warnings successful? What can early warning systems learn from these experiences?

- What should the global conflict early warning architecture look like in order to be able to prevent another Rwanda and manage future security threats? What regions need to be covered? What types of systems and groups should, in combination, comprise that cover?

- What are the cumulative key lessons learned in conflict early response – particularly in the involvement of different agencies, mechanisms/instruments, and operational and structural measures?

- What is the true nature of weak political will to respond? What are its constituent parts? And what strategies should be deployed to address them? How can accountability in responses be bolstered?

- What is the "lay of the land" in current regional and international institutions involved in responding to violent conflict and state failure? What does the broad picture – institutional base, response mechanisms/instruments, and operational/structural measures – look like?

Recommendations for the OECD DAC

This report concludes with key recommendations for the OECD DAC on how to support effective early warning and early response efforts.

1. Assist in the consolidation of good (quantitative and qualitative) methodological and applied reporting practice for conflict analysis and state fragility analysis.

The consolidation of good methodological practice needs to focus on both methods and their application (see Chapters 1 and 2). It needs to include the following:

- The organisation of a conflict and state fragility analysis workshop that brings together method developers to discuss and document good practice. Topics covered should include how different (quantitative and qualitative) methods can best be combined to yield a more robust evidence base for decision making.

- Increased funding of efforts to develop more applied qualitative state fragility assessments – particularly as these relate to institutional planning cycles and impact assessments of efforts to reduce state fragility. This is a very new area and the DAC may have a comparative advantage here.

- Explore further (through applied research) how state fragility indices or assessments can be used to better inform resource allocations and what their limitations are for that purpose. This would entail expanding the DAC work on monitoring resource allocation by monitoring how resources are allocated in relation to state fragility – and the strengths/weaknesses of basing resource allocations on "watch list"-type assessments.

- Prepare a short DAC "recommended reporting standards" document for conflict analysis, early warning and state fragility reports, and disseminate these broadly as part of ensuring improved reporting on violent conflict and state fragility. Such reporting standards will provide important benchmarks for early warners to attain, and will help improve how analytical methods are applied.

- Concretely outline the critical importance of adopting innovative information communication technologies for data collection, communication, visualisation and analysis.

2. Consider how early warning systems can promote improved understanding of armed violence dynamics (see Chapter 4).

- An indicator list based on case studies is required to help identify what factors early warners need to analyse when operating systems in areas affected by armed violence. Such (non-prescriptive) indicators should include those related to, *inter alia,* the political economy of violence and supply and demand of weapons.

- More sophisticated methods for stakeholder analysis are required to capture group motivations (beyond grievance) and relationships, especially given the importance of group and leadership culture and psychology in violent conflict situations.

3. Consider the need for a bolstered global early global early warning and response architecture (see Chapters 2, 3 and 4).

- Consider how a shared, diversified and more robust evidence base for decision making on violent conflict and state fragility can be created – particularly in view of the reduced number of global sources of analysis and the need to align current early warning systems (and funding pools) with political (as opposed to developmental) decision makers. Explore the establishment of a new global network for early warning and response (involving regional organisations, governments, and non-governmental agencies) to address this deficit.

- Endorse efforts to build internal capacity and functional external relations among staff dealing with conflict-affected countries and situations of state fragility. Capacity building needs to involve skills development, and internal reviews of existing institutional processes that enable (or disable) officials from pursuing appropriate and rapid responses.

- Promote the practice of regular assessments of "whole-of-system" responses to violent conflict and state fragility situations (along the lines of the Rwanda Joint Evaluation) to build the knowledge base from the applied "do's and don'ts". Ensure that the reviews both tackle the institutional mechanism/instrument and measures dimensions of responses.

- Call for the standard use of multi-stakeholder platforms for joint problem definition and planning of responses to situations of violent conflict and state fragility. Ensure that such platforms include both state and civil society groups, along with regional and international organisations.

- Consider how well placed (or not) current regional and international early warning and response capabilities are to assess and respond to global current and future security threats. This could involve calling for a high-level meeting to review the current global conflict early warning and response architecture.

4. Increase support for regional early warning systems, and third generation systems that address micro-level violence.

There is a need to invest more effectively in conflict early warning systems. Such investment should be focused on the early warning efforts of regional organisations and those of non-governmental organisations that fall into the category of third generation systems (see Chapters 1 and 2).

- Investments in the early warning efforts of regional organisations need to focus on bolstering: *(a)* the quality of reporting; *(b)* the warning-response link; and *(c)* sensitivity among senior policy making of the value of evidence-based decision making in situations of violent conflict and state fragility.

- Investments in third generation systems need to be focused on strengthening the institutional capacities of operating organisations. This needs to include core funding for permanent staff, funding for capacity building, access to technology, and other network running costs.

- All regional and third generation systems need to be encouraged to consider how their efforts could be adjusted to enable analysis and response to future security threats. Bringing these groups together onto a broad global platform can also facilitate the exchange of lessons learned and cross-fertilisation of good practice.

Bibliography

Adelman, H. (2006), "The War Report: Warning And Response in West Africa", USAID/WARP (Accra), February.

Aga Khan, S. (1981), "Question of the Violation of Human Rights and Fundamental Freedoms in any Part of the World, with Particular Reference to Colonial and Other Dependent Countries and Territories" in *Study on Human Rights and Massive Exodus,* United Nations Economic and Social Council, Commission on Human Rights, 38th Session, Item 12 (b), E1CN1411503, 31 December.

Anderson, M.B, (1999), Do no harm: How Aid Can Support Peace – Or War. Lynne Rienner Pub, Boulder, Colorado.

Austin, G., E. Brusset, M. Chalmers and J. Pierce (2004), *Evaluation of the Conflict Prevention Pools: Synthesis Report,* DFID, London.

Banim, G. (2008) "EU Responses to Fragile States" in Stefani Weiss, Hans-Joachim Spanger, Wim van Meurs (eds.), *Diplomacy, Development and Defence: A Paradigm for Policy Coherence, A Comparative Analysis of International Strategies*, Verlag Bertelsmann Stiftung, Guetersloh.

Barrs, C. (2006), "Conflict Early Warning: Early Warning for Who?", *Journal of Humanitarian Assistance,* February.

Barrs, C. (2008), *Preparedness Training: Helping Brace Beneficiaries, Local Staff and Partners for Violence*, The Cuny Center, Washington, DC.

Cammack, D., D. McLeod, A. Rocha Menocal and K. Christiansen (2006), *Donors and the "Fragile States" Agenda: A Survey of Current Thinking and Practice,* ODI/JICA, London.

Campbell, S. and P. Meier (2007), "Deciding to Prevent Violent Conflict: Early Warning and Decision-Making at the United Nations", Paper presented at the International Studies Association (ISA) Convention, Chicago, March.

Carment, D., Y. Samy and S. Prest (2007), "Determinants of State Fragility and Implications for Aid Allocation: An Assessment", CIFP, Carleton University, Ottawa, May.

Carnegie Commission on Preventing Deadly Conflict (1997), Final Report, New York, December.

Cewarn (2006), *Cewarn Strategy 2007-2011.* Cewarn Unit, Addis Abeba, November.

Charney, I. and W. Charney (1982), "How Can We Commit the Unthinkable?" in *Genocide – The Human Cancer,* Westview Press, Boulder, Colorado.

Cilliers, J. (2005), "Towards a Continental Early Warning System for Africa", Occasional Paper 102, ISS, April.

European Commission (2001), *Communication from the Commission on Conflict Prevention.* Brussels, July.

European Commission (2008), "Climate Change And International Security", Paper from the High Representative and the European Commission to the European Council, S113/08, Brussels, March.

European Parliament (2008), *Options for the EU to Support the African Peace and Security Architecture,* European Parliament, Policy Department External Policies, EP/EXPO/B/AFET/FWC/2006-10/Lot 4/13, Brussels, February.

Fall, I. (2008), "Coopération opérationelle entre organisations internationales en matière de l'alerte précoce et de prévention des conflits", Paper presented to the OIF Meeting on Early Warning and Conflict Prevention, Paris, 21-22 April.

Goldstone, J.A. (2008), "Using Quantitative and Qualitative Models to Forecast Instability", Special Report 204, US Institute of Peace, March.

Hopkins, D. and G. King (2008), "Extracting Systematic Social Science Meaning from Text", Institute for Quantitative Social Science (IQSS), Harvard University.

IGAD (Inter-Governmental Authority on Development) (2000), "Khartoum Declaration of the Eighth IGAD Summit", Khartoum, 23 November.

Lavoix, H. (2007), *Etude sur l'Alerte Précoce,* Ministère des Affaires Etrangères, Paris.

Leaning, J. and P. Meier (2008), *The Untapped Potential of Information Communication Technology for Conflict Early Warning and Early Response*, Harvard Humanitarian Initiative (HHI) Report for Humanity United, Harvard University.

Matveeva, A. (2006), *Early Warning and Early Response: Conceptual and Empirical Dilemmas,* GPAC Issue Paper No. 1, September.

Netherlands Ministry for Foreign Affairs (2005), *The Stability Assessment Framework: Designing Integrated Responses for Security, Governance and Development,* The Hague.

Nyheim, D. (2003), "What Can Be Done?" in Carol Rittner, John K. Roth and James M. Smith (eds.), *Will Genocide Ever End?*, Paragon House.

OECD (2001), *DAC Guidelines on Conflict, Peace and Development Co-operation*, OECD, Paris. (1ˢᵗ edition in 1997).

OECD (2008), *Thematic Meetings on Whole-of-Government Approaches to Situations of Conflict and Fragility,* OECD, Paris, May.

Ogata, S. and A. Sen (2003), *Human Security Now*, May.

PCIA Resource Pack (2004), *Conflict Sensitive Approaches to Development, Humanitarian Assistance and Peacebuilding: A Resource Pack,* London, January.

Rice, S. and P. Stewart (2008), *Index of State Weakness in the Developing World,* Brookings Institution.

Rupesinghe, K. (1989), "Early Warning: Some Conceptual Problems", *Bulletin of Peace Proposals,* 20, 2.

Schimd, A. (1998), *Thesaurus and Glossary of Early Warning and Conflict Prevention Terms (Abridged Version)*, FEWER/PIOOM.

Schmeidl, S. (2008), "Early Warning at the Grassroots Level", Paper presented at the International Studies Association (ISA) Convention, San Francisco, March.

Schmeidl, S. and E. Piza-Lopez (2002), *Gender and Conflict Early Warning: A Framework for Action,* International Alert, London.

Singer, J.D. and M.D. Wallace, eds. (1979), *To Augur Well: Early Warning Indicators in World Politics*, Sage Focus Editions, Sage Publications, Inc.

Slim, H. (2006), *Towards Some Ethical Guidelines for Good Practice in Third Party Mediation in Armed Conflict,* Oslo Forum, Oslo.

Smith, D. (2003), *Getting Their Act Together: Towards a Strategic Framework for Peacebuilding* (Synthesis Report of the Joint Utstein

Study of Peacebuilding), Commissioned by the Royal Norwegian Ministry of Foreign Affairs, Oslo.

Sriram, C.L. and K. Wermester (2003), *From Promise to Practice: Strengthening UN Capacities for the Prevention of Violent Conflict: Final Report,* International Peace Academy, New York, March.

Steering Committee of the Joint Evaluation of Emergency Assistance to Rwanda (1996), *The International Response to Conflict and Genocide: Lessons from the Rwanda Experience,* March.

swisspeace (2005), "FAST Update: Russian Federation/Chechnya", Semi-annual Risk Assessment, November 2004 to February 2005, *www.swisspeace.ch/typo3/fileadmin/user_upload/pdf/FAST/archive/nort h_caucasus/FAST-FEWER_Update_Chech_Nov04-Feb05.pdf.*

swisspeace (2007), "FAST Update Afghanistan No. 4", August to September 2007.

Taleb, N. (2007), *The Black Swan: The Impact of the Highly Improbable,* Random House, New York.

Teslik, L.H. (2008), "Iraq, Afghanistan, and the U.S. Economy", Council on Foreign Relations, March.

United Kingdom Government (2000), *Eliminating World Poverty: Making Globalisation Work for the Poor,* Government White Paper, London.

United Nations (1992), "An Agenda for Peace Preventive Diplomacy, Peacemaking and Peace-keeping", Report of the Secretary-General pursuant to the statement adopted by the Summit Meeting of the Security Council on 31 January 1992, A/47/277 - S/24111, New York, 17 June.

United Nations (2000), "Report of the Panel on United Nations Peace Operations", New York.

United Nations (2001), "Prevention of Armed Conflict Report of the Secretary-General", General Assembly Fifty-fifth Session, Agenda Item 10, A/55/985–S/2001/574, New York.

Woocher, L. (2007), "Early Warning for the Prevention of Genocide and Mass Atrocities", Paper presented at the International Studies Association (ISA) Convention, Chicago, March.

World Bank (2006), *Engaging with Fragile States,* World Bank, Washington, DC.

Zeeuw, J. de (2001) *Building Peace in War Torn Societies: From Concept to Strategy*, Netherlands Institute of International Relations "Clingendael", Conflict Research Unit.

Annex

Compendium of Surveyed Early Warning Systems and Early Response Mechanisms/Instruments

This compendium summarises questionnaires completed by different agencies as part of an OECD DAC mapping exercise of early warning and early response systems (December 2007 to May 2008). Where relevant, it also draws on information from other reviews of early warning systems (e.g. Cilliers, 2005; Lavoix, 2007), as well as other institutional documents available from respondents. The compendium does not include details of early warning systems/response mechanisms and instruments where respondents were unable to complete questionnaires. It serves as a supplement to the present OECD/DAC report Preventing Violence, War and State Collapse: The Future of Conflict Early Warning and Response. *The compendium is organised into governmental, inter-governmental and non-governmental early warning systems and response mechanisms/instruments. The different warning systems and response mechanism/instruments covered are described in brief profiles.*

Early warning systems

Governmental early warning efforts

France - *Système d'Alerte Précoce*

Agency name	*Secrétariat général de la défense nationale - Direction des affaires internationales et stratégiques* - SAP
Type of EWS	Qualitative HQ based Governmental system
EWS objective and focus	Objective: Monitor and alert decision makers on violent conflict, political instability, and state fragility in countries covered Focus: 25 countries where French interests are significant
Legal basis (if any)	N/A
Annual budget and donor	N/A
Geographical/ operational scope	Geographical scope: 25 countries in Africa, Latin America, South Asia, Central Asia and the Caucasus Operational scope: Fragile states at risk of instability over the next 24 months
Activities and methodology	Activities: Monitoring and watch listing Analytical methodology used: Qualitative (details unavailable) Information sources used: Open sources and closed sources (diplomatic and intelligence)
Warning products	Warning products and frequency: Monthly syntheses and annual reports Target audience: Ministers, their cabinets, and director-level decision makers of agencies that can respond to crises
Institutional set-up	SAP is located in the *Secrétariat général de la défense nationale - Direction des affaires internationales et stratégiques*
Linkages with response	Analyses are disseminated to key decision makers
Co-operation, co-ordination and partnerships	Part of inter-ministerial working group (seven ministries involved)

Germany – BMZ Crisis Early Warning System*

Agency name	BMZ – Crisis Early Warning System
Type of EWS	Qualitative with quantitative component HQ based Combined system: Government and think tank
EWS objective and focus	Objective: Inform development programming in crisis-affected countries Focus: Countries affected by crisis and violent conflict
Legal basis (if any)	N/A
Annual budget and donor	N/A
Geographical/ operational scope	Geographical scope: 80-100 countries of interest to BMZ Operational scope: Crisis and violent conflict
Activities and methodology	Activities: Informational collection and analysis – first by external group (GIGA) then by internal desk officers Analytical methodology used: Qualitative questionnaire with quantitative scoring element Information sources used: Open sources
Warning products	Warning products and frequency: Annual analysis and watch list Target audience: Desk officers within BMZ and related government agencies
Institutional set-up	The analysis of the BMZ system is driven initially by GIGA, and then transmitted to BMZ desk officers for internal analysis and verification
Linkages with response	Work on early warning feeds into the BMZ strategic concept on crisis prevention and peace building. For countries with heightened and acute prevention needs, a conflict-sensitive design of the country portfolio and its programmes is ensured
Co-operation, co-ordination and partnerships	Co-operation with other departments and ministries of the German government

*Profile draws on material from Lavoix, 2007.

United States – State Department and National Intelligence Council – Instability Watch List*

Agency name	SD/NIC – Instability Watch List
Type of EWS	Quantitative HQ based Governmental system
EWS objective and focus	Objective: Identify countries at risk of instability
Legal basis (if any)	N/A
Annual budget and donor	N/A
Geographical/ operational scope	Geographical scope: N/A Operational scope: Political instability
Activities and methodology	Activities: Preparation of Watch List Analytical methodology used: PITF quantitative methodology Information sources used: Open and closed sources
Warning products	Warning products and frequency: Annual Watch List Target audience: Government decision makers
Institutional set-up	The Instability Watch List is jointly used by the State Department and National Intelligence Council
Linkages with response	N/A
Co-operation, co-ordination and partnerships	N/A

*Profile draws on material from Lavoix, 2007.

Inter-governmental early warning efforts

African Union – Continental Early Warning System*

Agency name	African Union – CEWS
Type of EWS	Qualitative HQ based Combined system: Multilateral and civil society
EWS objective and focus	Objective: Advise the Council on "potential conflicts and threats to peace and security" and "recommend best courses of action"
Legal basis (if any)	Various, including the Central Mechanism for Conflict Prevention, Management and Resolution (1993), and Peace and Security Council Protocol (2003)
Annual budget and donor	N/A
Geographical/ operational scope	Geographical scope: Africa Operational scope: Violent conflict, threats to peace and security
Activities and methodology	Activities: Information collection, analysis, briefings and dissemination Analytical methodology used: Generic and specific indicators related to DFID's Strategic Conflict Assessment methodology Information sources used: Media, reports from regional EWS, other sources
Warning products	Warning products and frequency: Special Early Warning Reports; Recommendations for the AU Commission President and PSC President; Regional Reports updated 2-3 times yearly; News Highlights, Mission Reports, and Chairperson's Reports Target audience: AU Commission, PSC, Panel of the Wise, Pan-African Parliament, other internal decision makers
Institutional set-up	Set within the Peace and Security Council
Linkages with response	Links to internal AU decision makers, as well as decision makers in other bodies
Co-operation, co-ordination and partnerships	Regional Organisations (ECOWAS, SADC, IGAD, etc.), UN Secretariat and its agencies, civil society groups

*Profile draws on material from Lavoix, 2007 and Cilliers, 2005.

Economic Community of Central African States – *Mechanisme d'Alerte Rapide pour l'Afrique Centrale* (MARAC)

Agency name	ECCAS – MARAC
Type of EWS	Qualitative and quantitative HQ based (field monitors to be deployed) Combined system: Multilateral and civil society
EWS objective and focus	Objective: Prevent, manage and settle conflicts; and reduce the sources of tensions and prevent the eruption of armed conflicts Focus: ECCAS member states
Legal basis (if any)	"Peace and Security Council for Central Africa" (COPAX) (1999)
Annual budget and donor	N/A – but funded from member states and the European Union
Geographical/ operational scope	Geographical scope: Central Africa (ECCAS member states) Operational scope: Prevention of violent conflicts
Activities and methodology	Activities: Information collection, analysis, and recommendations for response provided to decision makers Analytical methodology used: Qualitative and quantitative (details unavailable) Information sources used: Open source reports and local monitors (forthcoming)
Warning products	Warning products and frequency (forthcoming): Daily news flash, weekly reviews, annual report Target audience: ECCAS decision makers, expanded later to include ECCAS member state officials
Institutional set-up	MARAC falls under the Commission for Defence and Security (CDS) and is one of two instruments for prevention, the other being a Multinational Peace Keeping Force in Central Africa (FOMAC)
Linkages with response	Analyses will be transmitted to decision makers at different levels
Co-operation, co-ordination and partnerships	Co-operation with the AU, other regional organisations, and NGOs

ECOWAS - ECOWARN

Agency name	ECOWAS – ECOWARN
Type of EWS	Quantitative and qualitative Field based and HQ based Combined system: Government, multilateral and civil society
EWS objective and focus	Objective: To engage in data collection and analysis, and the drafting of up-to-date reports on possible emerging crises, ongoing crises and post-crisis transitions Focus: Violent conflicts, political instability, state fragility, human rights violations, and human security in the ECOWAS region
Legal basis (if any)	ECOWAS Protocol Relating to the Mechanism for Conflict Prevention, Management, Resolution, Peacekeeping and Security (1999)
Annual budget and donor	USD 2 million (approximately EUR 1.3 million), ECOWAS, USAID, Africa Peace Facility (African Union), and African Development Bank (ADB)
Geographical/ operational scope	Geographical scope: Fifteen member states of ECOWAS
Activities and methodology	Activities: Monitoring and data collection, incident and situation reporting (soon to evolve into comprehensive monthly, quarterly and annual reporting) Analytical methodology used: Field monitoring and (quantitative) data collection by monitors through a database; data analysis and reporting/formulation of response options using qualitative WARN/FEWER conflict analysis methodology Information sources used: Media and local field monitors
Warning products	Warning products and frequency: Daily highlights, reports, policy briefs (currently *ad hoc* but soon regular) Target audience: ECOWAS (sub-regional economic community); national governments and international community
Institutional set-up	ECOWARN is located in the Office of the Commissioner for Political Affairs, Peace and Security (PAPS)
Linkages with response	Connections within ECOWAS to different response mechanisms
Co-operation, co-ordination and partnerships	Co-operates with AU and other regional organisations. Operational partnership with WANEP, a regional non-governmental organisation since 2002. WANEP serves as implementing partner alongside member states through technical support in data collection and analysis

European Union – EU Watch List

Agency name	European Commission and Council of Ministers (Policy Planning and Early Warning Unit)
Type of EWS	Qualitative HQ based Combined system: Multilateral and governmental
EWS objective and focus	Objective: Identify and monitor countries at risk of violent conflict, political instability, and state fragility and stimulate debate among EU foreign ministries on how the EU can best respond to these issues
Legal basis (if any)	Part of the ongoing development of the Common Foreign and Security Policy (CFSP) since its inception in the Maastricht Treaty (1993)
Annual budget and donor	NA
Geographical/ operational scope	Geographical scope: Global (except EU member states and close partners) Operational scope: Violent conflict, political instability, state fragility/collapse, security, social instability, organised crime, and terrorism
Activities and methodology	Activities: Preparation of a six-monthly EU Watch List Analytical methodology used: European Commission uses a cluster analysis and a proprietary set of qualitative and quantitative variables to provide a reference to desk officers for their assessment. The Watch List is consensus based and involved collaboration between the SITCEN, the Policy Unit, the EU Military Staff and DG RELEX Information sources used: Member states, EU special representatives, EC delegations and other representatives of the Commission, as well as the Council Secretariat, including the Policy Unit and the EU Military Staff (EUMS)
Warning products	Warning products and frequency: Six-monthly Watch List Target audience: EU member state and institutions decision makers
Institutional set-up	Linked to the CFSP Committees and involving SITCEN, the Policy Unit, the EU Military Staff and DG RELEX
Linkages with response	The Watch List is presented for approval without recommendations for response. It is used when setting up the agenda for meetings of the PSC ambassadors or geographical working groups
Co-operation, co-ordination and partnerships	Exchange of views occurs mainly with the UN and some of its agencies, OSCE, member states and some field-based NGOs

IGAD - Conflict Early Warning and Response Mechanism (CEWARN)

Agency name	IGAD – CEWARN
Type of EWS	Qualitative and quantitative Field based and HQ based Combined system: Government, multilateral and civil society
EWS objective and focus	Objective: Mandate is to "receive and share information concerning potentially violent conflicts as well as their outbreak and escalation in the IGAD region." Focus: Pastoralist and related conflicts
Legal basis (if any)	IGAD's CEWARN Protocol (January 2002)
Annual budget and donor	USD 1.4 million (approximately EUR 900 000), USAID, GTZ, and member states
Geographical/ operational scope	Geographical scope: The Karamoja Cluster (cross-border areas of Ethiopia, Kenya, Sudan and Uganda), the Somali Cluster (cross-border areas of Ethiopia, Kenya and Somalia), and the Afar/Issa Cluster (cross-border region of Djibouti and Eritrea)
Activities and methodology	Activities: Monitoring and reporting, providing response options Analytical methodology used: Data-based monitoring using CEWARN Reporter software. The software assists in analysis of data collected, is based on 52 indicators, includes structural data, climatic/environmental data Information sources used: Local field monitors, media sources
Warning products	Warning products and frequency: Alerts (as they occur), regional cluster reports (quarterly), monthly updates (monthly), and situational reports Target audience: Decision makers in the IGAD region
Institutional set-up	CEWARN falls under the Peace and Security Division of the IGAD Secretariat. Its policy organs are the Committee of Permanent Secretaries and the Technical Committee on Early Warning and Response
Linkages with response	Conflict Early Warning and Early Response Units (CEWERUs) at local and national level in member states
Co-operation, co-ordination and partnerships	Co-operates with AU and other regional organisations. Donor partners include USAID and GTZ. Partnerships with civil society organisations in the Horn of Africa, and academic institutions

United Nations – Various Systems

Agency name	United Nations – Various Systems • OCHA – Early Warning Unit (New York) • OCHA – Humanitarian Situation Room (Colombia) • UNDP – Country-level early warning systems in Ghana, Kenya, Ukraine (Crimea), Bolivia, Balkans, and Kyrgyzstan
Type of EWS	Qualitative • Field based and HQ based • Combined system: Multilateral and civil society
EWS objective and focus	Objectives: To inform humanitarian contingency planning efforts for complex emergencies To inform country programming of UN agencies and partners Focus: Violent conflicts, political instability, state fragility, and human security in countries covered
Legal basis (if any)	N/A – But follow from recommendations in "An Agenda for Peace" (1992); "Report of the Panel on United Nations Peace Operations" (2000); and "Prevention of Armed Conflict: Report of the Secretary-General" (2001)
Annual budget and donor	N/A
Geographical/ operational scope	Geographical scope: Global and country-specific
Activities and methodology	Activities: Monitoring and data collection, briefings and reporting Analytical methodology used: Various. Ranges from indicator checklists and social science research methods (including surveys, etc.) to basic qualitative conflict analysis methods Information sources used: Various field missions, media and local sources
Warning products	Warning products and frequency: Various. Ranges from *ad hoc* briefings and reports, to regular situation briefs and annual reports Target audience: UN agency decision makers and partners
Institutional set-up	Various – but linked to UNOCHA, UNDP, and DPA
Linkages with response	Linked at technical level to Framework Team that elaborates inter-agency responses to early warnings received
Co-operation, co-ordination and partnerships	Inter-agency partnership through the Framework Team. Co-operation between different early warning systems and civil society groups in countries covered

Non-governmental early warning efforts

BELUN/CICR – Early Warning and Early Response Project (EWER)

Agency name	BELUN and Columbia University's Center for International Conflict Resolution (CICR)
Type of EWS	Qualitative and Quantitative Field based and HQ based Community-based system
EWS objective and focus	Objective: two-pronged approach integrating early warning/response strategies and tactics for state-level institutions and local communities respectively to prevent escalation of community-based violence Focus: Timor-Leste
Legal basis (if any)	N/A
Annual budget and donor	Budget: EUR 10 000 (Phase 1 only) Main donors: International Forum for Election Systems (IFES)
Geographical/ operational scope	Geographical scope: Timor-Leste Operational scope: Prevention of violence, preparedness training
Activities and methodology	Activities: *(a)* Monitoring and information collection; *(b)* analysis and report preparation; *(c)* dissemination of reports; (d) tactical preparedness training; *(d)* conflict management training; *(e)* early response fund Analytical methodology used: incident report and situation reporting Information sources used: Local monitors and communities and structural conflict assessments
Warning products	TBD, EWER completed Phase 1. Applying for funding to implement Phases 2 and 3.
Institutional set-up	BELUN (Timor-Leste's only national NGO)
Linkages with response	Reports and briefings directly to key decision makers
Co-operation, co-ordination and partnerships	Close co-operation with local civil society networks and state institutions; Harvard Humanitarian Initiative (HHI)

FEWER-Africa – Ituri Watch

Agency name	FEWER-Africa - IW
Type of EWS	Qualitative Field based and HQ based Civil society system
EWS objective and focus	Objective: To prevent inter-community violence and promote reintegration of combatants in Ituri Province (DRC) Focus: Ituri Province (DRC)
Legal basis (if any)	N/A
Annual budget and donor	Budget: EUR 50 000 Main donors: FEWER-Africa core funds
Geographical/ operational scope	Geographical scope: Ituri Province Operational scope: Prevention of violence
Activities and methodology	Activities: *(a)* Monitoring and information collection; *(b)* analysis and report preparation; and *(c)* dissemination of reports Analytical methodology used: FEWER qualitative conflict analysis methodology Information sources used: Local monitors, media and structural data sources
Warning products	Warning products and frequency: Monthly monitoring report, briefings Target audience: DRC government decision makers, local authorities and leaders, international community
Institutional set-up	FEWER-Africa hosts Ituri Watch
Linkages with response	Reports and briefings directly to key decision makers
Co-operation, co-ordination and partnerships	Close co-operation with local civil society networks

FEWER-Eurasia

Agency name	FEWER-Eurasia
Type of EWS	Qualitative and Quantitative Field based and HQ based Civil society system
EWS objective and focus	Objective: To provide information and analysis for conflict prevention and to respond to crisis in the North Caucasus Focus: Republic level in the Russian Federation
Legal basis (if any)	N/A
Annual budget and donor	Budget: USD 250 000 (approximately EUR 160 000) Main donors : Swiss Federal Department for Foreign Affairs, Swedish Ministry of Foreign Affairs
Geographical/ operational scope	Geographical scope: North Caucasian republics (Dagestan, Chechnya, Ingushetia, North-Ossetia-Alania, Karachay-Cherkess, Kabardin-Balkar) Operational scope: Prevention of violence and peacebuilding
Activities and methodology	Activities: Monitoring, briefings, report writing, and database development Analytical methodology used: A combination of EAWARN, FEWER, FAST/swisspeace, and IDEA indicator-based models Information sources used: Media at all levels, NGO bulletins and reports, network of local monitors/experts
Warning products	Warning products and frequency: Bi-monthly republic-level updates and yearly reports Target audience: Russian government decision makers, donor governments, international organisations, and humanitarian agencies
Institutional set-up	FEWER-Eurasia works closely with General Lebed's Peace Mission and EAWARN
Linkages with response	Warning efforts feed directly into activities on fostering humanitarian multi-stakeholder dialogue that brings together Russian government decision makers at all levels and civil society, as well as international partners
Co-operation, Co-ordination and partnerships	swisspeace, EAWARN (information exchange)

Foundation for Co-Existence – Programme on Human Security and Co-Existence

Agency name	FCE – PHSC
Type of EWS	Qualitative and quantitative Field based and HQ based Civil society system
EWS objective and focus	Objective: To promote human security in Sri Lanka Focus: Provincial and district levels
Legal basis (if any)	N/A
Annual budget and donor	Budget: USD 350 000 (approximately EUR 225 000) Main donors: The British High Commission in Sri Lanka, The Royal Norwegian Embassy in Sri Lanka, and the World Bank
Geographical/ operational scope	Geographical scope: Eastern, Northern, Central and Western Provinces; Trincaomalee, Batticaloa, Ampara , Mannar, Nuwara Eliya districts and Colombo slum dwellings. Operational scope: Prevention of violence and promotion of human security
Activities and methodology	Activities: *(a)* Situation monitoring in conflict zones; *(b)* coding events data into INFO SYS software and Geographic Mapping System (GIS); *(c)* analysis of information at local and HQ levels; *(d)* identification of potential risks/violence/threats to human security; *(e)* early/rapid response interventions to prevent conflicts; *(f)* preparation of reports; *(g)* monthly roundtable briefings; and *(h)* local level meetings Analytical methodology used: Events Data Collection Methodology; quantitative (FAST methodology adapted to local level) and qualitative conflict analysis Information sources used: Local field monitors, media, websites and structural data
Warning products	Warning products and frequency: Daily situation reports, weekly analysis reports, monthly risk assessments and special reports/case studies Target audience: Local actors, national and international decision makers
Institutional set-up	PHSC is a programme of the FCE
Linkages with response	Analyses are transmitted to decision makers at different levels through reports and briefings Rapid response mechanisms are in place and involve local monitors and formal inter-ethnic associations called Co-Existence Committees (CECs) that respond to warnings
Co-operation, co-ordination and partnerships	N/A

Foundation for Tolerance International – Early Warning and Violence Prevention Project

Agency name	FTI-EWVPP
Type of EWS	Qualitative and quantitative Field based and HQ based Combined civil society and multilateral system
EWS objective and focus	Objective: To provide information and analysis for conflict prevention in Kyrgyzstan and neighbouring countries Focus: Kyrgyzstan and border areas
Legal basis (if any)	N/A
Annual budget and donor	Budget: EUR 116 000 Main donors: Belgian Ministry of Foreign Affairs
Geographical/ operational scope	Geographical scope: Kyrgyzstan and borders Operational scope: Prevention of violence and peacebuilding
Activities and methodology	Activities: *(a)* Monitoring of the overall situation in the state; *(b)* dissemination of information on and analyses of violent conflicts and conflicts with high violence potential; and *(c)* coaching, training and workshops on conflict/violence prevention Analytical methodology used: Qualitative conflict analysis Information sources used: Local monitors, decision makers, conflict parties, media and law enforcement agencies
Warning products	Warning products and frequency: Weekly bulletin, special analytical notes (confidential) for key decision makers and/or conflicting parties, thematic studies and practical guidelines Target audience: Conflicting parties, decision makers in the government, local authorities, and the expert community
Institutional set-up	FTI hosts the EWVPP
Linkages with response	Warnings and recommendations are provided directly to decision makers and conflicting parties
Co-operation, co-ordination and partnerships	FTI/EWVPP works closely with state structures, NGOs and law enforcement agencies

Institute for Security Studies – African Security Analysis Programme (ASAP)

Agency name	ISS-ASAP
Type of EWS	Qualitative HQ based NGO system
EWS objective and focus	Objectives: Track and monitor threats to human security in the five geographical regions of the continent Undertake in-depth desk and field research into factors that impact on human security in Africa Contribute to a better understanding of instability factors Focus: Violent conflict and war; humanitarian interventions; post-conflict reconstruction, rehabilitation, reintegration, reconciliation; democracy, good governance, and human rights; African armed forces; African peace and security architecture; demobilisation, disarmament and reintegration; security sector reform; elections; and state fragility
Legal basis (if any)	N/A
Annual budget and donor	Budget: ZAR 750 000 (approximately EUR 65 000) Main donors: Norway, Sweden, Finland, Denmark, Switzerland and Germany
Geographical/operational scope	Geographical scope: Africa Operational scope: Fragile states
Activities and methodology	Activities: (a) Monitoring of conflict situations and threats to human security in the continent; (b) production of briefings (oral and written) to assess risks; (c) seminars and conferences; (d) media interaction; (e) support to the African Union's Continental Early Warning System (CEWS); (f) interaction with the Pan-African Parliament; and (g) lectures and training courses Analytical methodology used: Desk and field research, data analysis, and expert judgement Information sources used: Open source, primary and secondary data, interaction with decision makers
Warning products	Warning products and frequency: Oral briefings (daily) that take place in the ASAP Situation Room; written notes of these briefings (daily); situation reports (quarterly); occasional papers, monographs and books; briefing notes on request (occasional); and seminars and roundtables (monthly). Target audience: Government decision makers, regional organisations (AU and others), research and policy organisations, practitioners, NGOs, and western donors
Institutional set-up	ASAP is housed by ISS
Linkages with response	Formal and non-formal linkages to decision makers in target audience institutions
Co-operation, co-ordination and partnerships	Close co-operation with regional organisations, governments, and NGOs/think tanks

Swisspeace - Early Recognition and Analysis of Tensions (FAST) (now closed)

Agency name	swisspeace – FAST
Type of EWS	Qualitative and quantitative Field based and HQ based NGO system
EWS objective and focus	Objective: To provide information and analysis for conflict prevention and conflict-sensitive development programming Focus: Priority countries of donor agencies
Legal basis (if any)	N/A
Annual budget and donor	Budget: CHF 1.8 million (approximately EUR 1.1 million) Main donors: SDC, SIDA, CIDA, ADA
Geographical/ operational scope	Geographical scope: Horn of Africa, Great Lakes, South Africa, Central Asia, South Asia, Caucasus, and Balkans Operational scope: Prevention of violence and peacebuilding
Activities and methodology	Activities: Monitoring, bi-monthly risk assessments, in-depth country reports, occasional briefings Analytical methodology used: Event data analysis combined with qualitative expert judgement Information sources used: Local networks and expert know-how
Warning products	Warning products and frequency: Bi-monthly risk assessments and country reports Target audience: Desk officers in development agencies
Institutional set-up	FAST was a programme of swisspeace
Linkages with response	Tailored recommendations provided to client agencies
Co-operation, co-ordination and partnerships	Co-operation with FEWER Eurasia, WANEP, HURDEC, and ISS

Tribal Liaison Office (TLO) – Community-based Conflict Early Warning Project

Agency name	TLO
Type of EWS	Qualitative and quantitative Field based and HQ based NGO system
EWS objective and focus	The initiative focuses specifically on human security, as opposed to the security of the Afghan state. To this end, the TLO seeks a "lower-level" entry-point, *i.e.* the low-intensity conflicts that mire Southern Afghanistan.
Legal basis (if any)	N/A
Annual budget and donor	Budget: N/A Main donors: N/A
Geographical/ operational scope	Geographical scope: South Afghanistan Operational scope: Prevention of violence and peacebuilding
Activities and methodology	Activities: TBD Analytical methodology used: Event data analysis combined with qualitative judgement Information sources used: Local networks
Warning products	TBD
Institutional set-up	TLO
Linkages with response	Community-based governance mechanisms (mainly *shuras* and *jirgas*) tasked with governing traditional communities
Co-operation, co-ordination and partnerships	TBD

Ushahidi – Crowd sourcing Crisis Information

Agency name	Ushahidi
Type of EWS	Crisis mapping NGO system
EWS objective and focus	The goal of Ushahidi is to facilitate better responses to crises, particularly humanitarian crises, by providing organisations with free web-based platforms that can collect, map, and share data relating to a particular crisis. Ushahidi was developed during the post-election crisis in Kenya, where the tool was used to document incidents of violence as well as peace initiatives.
Legal basis (if any)	501(c)(3) status application in process, registered as a non-profit organisation in Florida
Annual budget and donor	Budget: USD 300 000 Main donors: Humanity United, NetSquared
Geographical/ operational scope	Geographical scope: Originally Kenya, now global Operational scope: Mapping of crises situations
Activities and methodology	Activities: Crisis mapping Analytical methodology used: dynamic mapping of conflict data, fully geo-referenced and in real time Information sources used: Local networks, citizen journalists, NGOs
Warning products	Google Map of Kenya
Institutional set-up	NGO
Linkages with response	Provides information on ongoing response initiatives
Co-operation, co-ordination and partnerships	Currently working on integration with Frontline SMS, and on pilot phase with several local NGOs in Kenya and international NGOs

West Africa Network for Peace-Building – West Africa Warning and Response Network (WARN)

Agency name	WANEP-WARN
Type of EWS	See ECOWAS-ECOWARN above. Additional countries covered: Chad and Cameroon.

Early response mechanisms and instruments

Governmental response mechanisms and instruments

United Kingdom – Conflict Prevention Pool

Agency name	UK – CPP
Type of mechanism/ instrument	Conflict Prevention Pool (CPP) (whole-of-government co-ordinating mechanism and funding instrument) Other instruments include the Stabilisation Aid Fund, Global Opportunities Fund, and Country Offices (contingency planning)
Mechanism/ instrument objective	A global and regional reduction in conflict and its impact, through improved UK and international efforts to prevent, manage and resolve conflict, and to create the conditions required for effective state building and economic development
Legal basis	N/A – CPPs were established following a government-wide review of UK conflict prevention work in 2000
Annual Budget	GBP 112 million (2008-09) (approximately EUR 141 million)
Geographical/ operational scope	Geographical scope: Africa, Americas, Balkans, Middle East and North Africa, Russia and Commonwealth of Independent States (CIS), South Asia Operational scope : Includes security and small arms control, international capacity building
Institutional set-up	Managed jointly by the Foreign and Commonwealth Office (FCO), Ministry of Defence (MOD) and Department for International Development (DFID)
Deployment time frame	N/A
Documented impacts?	Evaluated in 2004. "The contribution of the CPPs to effective conflict prevention could be improved if they are backed by more consistent approaches to joint assessment and priority setting, by more determined pursuit of the multiplier effects and economies available from co-ordinated international responses, and by allocation of more administrative resources and staff trained appropriately in the associated processes" (Austin *et al.*, 2004)

Canada – Stabilisation and Reconstruction Task Force (START)/Global Peace and Security Fund (GPSF)

Agency name	Canada – START/GPSF
Type of mechanism/ instrument	Stabilisation and Reconstruction Task Force (START) (whole-of-government co-ordinating mechanism)
	Global Peace and Security Fund (GPSF) (funding instrument)
Mechanism/ instrument objective	START: *(a)* ensure timely, co-ordinated and effective responses to international crises (natural and human-made) requiring whole-of-government action; *(b)* plan and deliver coherent, effective conflict prevention and crisis response initiatives in states in transition, when Canadian interests are implicated; and *(c)* manage the Global Peace and Security Fund (GPSF).
	GPSF: Support peace processes and mediation efforts, develop transitional justice and reconciliation initiatives, build peace enforcement and peace operations capabilities, promote civilian protection strategies in humanitarian contexts, and reduce the impact of landmines, small arms and light weapons.
Legal basis	N/A
Annual Budget	CAD 142 million (2006-07) (approximately EUR 91 million)
Geographical/ operational scope	Geographical scope: Flexible, but currently covering Afghanistan, Pakistan, Haiti, Sudan, Colombia, Uganda, Lebanon, and Middle East. Operational scope: Post-conflict states, fragile states
Institutional set-up	Institutional location: START is a unit within the Department of Foreign Affairs and International Trade Canada. START manages the GPSF
Deployment time frame	N/A
Documented impacts	START plays a leadership role within the government of Canada in providing expert policy advice on a range of peace and security issues:
	Peace operations: Relevant and timely START advice was critical in Canadian engagement on Afghanistan, Haiti, Lebanon and Sudan
	Rule of law: Helped provide the intellectual underpinnings for an international justice rapid response capability
	Security system reform: Developed and co-ordinated Canada's security and justice strategy for Haiti
	Mediation: For northern Uganda, provided critical policy advice for mediation efforts involving the Lord's Resistance Army, and has begun to outline a policy framework for building Canadian mediation capacity
	Landmines: Provided whole-of-government policy co-ordination and leadership as Canada responded to its obligations under the Ottawa Convention banning anti-personnel mines
	Small arms and light weapons: Led the development of Canada's international policy on these weapons, which are responsible for over 500 000 deaths annually
	Civilian protection: Ensured that principles of international humanitarian law were effectively integrated into Canadian policy interventions and statements on Lebanon, the West Bank and Gaza, and provided intellectual leadership in the development of a Canadian policy approach to refugees and internally displaced persons from Iraq and Afghanistan

Inter-governmental organisations

ECOWAS – Mechanism for Conflict Prevention, Management, Resolution, Peacekeeping and Security

Agency name	ECOWAS Mechanism
Type of mechanism/ instrument	Political response, good offices, military response (peacekeeping)
Mechanism/ instrument objective	Selected objectives include: Prevent, manage and resolve internal and inter-state conflicts Strengthen co-operation in the areas of conflict prevention, early warning, peacekeeping operations, control of cross-border crime, international terrorism and proliferation of small arms and anti-personnel mines Maintain and consolidate peace, security and stability within the Community Establish institutions and formulate policies that would allow for the organisation and co-ordination of humanitarian relief missions Promote close co-operation between member states in the areas of preventive diplomacy and peacekeeping Constitute and deploy a civilian and military force to maintain or restore peace within the sub-region, whenever the need arises
Legal basis	1999 ECOWAS Protocol Relating to the Mechanism for Conflict Prevention, Management, Resolution, Peace-Keeping and Security
Annual Budget	N/A – but funded by Africa Peace Facility (EU), ECOWAS, United States and France
Geographical/ operational scope	Geographical scope: West Africa and Africa Operational scope: See objectives above
Institutional set-up	Linked to the Council of the Wise and Mediation and Security Council
Deployment time frame	Context specific, but has been deployed within one week
Documented impacts?	Interventions in Liberia, Guinea Bissau, Togo and Guinea

European Union/European Commission – Instrument for Stability

Agency name	EU/EC – Instrument for Stability
Type of mechanism/ instrument	Instrument for Stability (Funding instrument)
Mechanism/ instrument objective	Selected objectives include: • Respond urgently to the needs of countries threatened with or undergoing severe political instability or suffering from the effects of technological or natural disasters • Improve the links between First Pillar and Second Pillar operations • Streamline short-term crisis response efforts with long-term programmes
Legal basis	European Parliament and European Council, "Regulation Establishing an Instrument for Stability", EC Regulation No. 1717/2006, 15 November 2006
Annual Budget	EUR 100 million (2007)
Geographical/ operational scope	Geographical scope: Global Operational scope : Political crisis, instability, technological/natural disasters
Institutional set-up	Managed by the European Commission through the Directorate-General for External Relations
Deployment time frame	N/A
Documented impacts?	NA

IGAD – Conflict Early Warning and Early Response Unit/Rapid Response Fund

Agency name	IGAD – CEWERU/Rapid Response Fund
Type of mechanism/ instrument	CEWERU – country-level and local committees charged with catalysing responses to early warnings Rapid Response Fund – financing instrument
Mechanism/ instrument objective	CEWERU: Communicate recommendations on policy and response options to decision makers RRF: Finance short-term preventive measures in response to early warnings based on CEWERU recommendations
Legal basis	IGAD's CEWARN Protocol (January 2002)
Annual Budget	RRF: USD 1.7 million (approximately EUR 1.1 million) from SIDA, GTZ, Denmark, Austria, the United Kingdom, Italy
Geographical/ operational scope	Geographical scope: Karamoja Cluster (cross-border areas of Ethiopia, Kenya, Sudan and Uganda) and Somali Cluster (cross-border areas of Ethiopia, Kenya and Somalia) Operational scope: Pastoralist and related conflicts
Institutional set-up	CEWARN falls under the Peace and Security Division of the IGAD Secretariat. Its policy organs are the Committee of Permanent Secretaries and the Technical Committee on Early Warning and Response
Deployment time frame	N/A
Documented impacts	Various, including disarmament work and Pokot case (see Case Study 2 in main report)

United Nations – Interdepartmental Framework for Coordination of Preventive Action

Agency name	UN – Framework Team
Type of mechanism/ instrument	Interdepartmental Framework for Coordination of Preventive Action (inter-agency response co-ordination mechanism) Other instruments include UNDP SURGE Mechanism, UNDP Track 113, and UNDP Thematic Trust Fund
Mechanism/ instrument objective	Co-ordinate planning and operational activities among the humanitarian, peacekeeping and political sectors of the Secretariat
Legal basis	N/A
Annual Budget	N/A
Geographical/ operational scope	Geographical scope: Global Operational scope : Violent conflict, crisis, and political instability
Institutional set-up	Involves DPA, OCHA, DPKO, UNDP, OHCHR, UNICEF, UNHCR, WFP, FAO and WHO
Deployment time frame	N/A
Documented impacts	N/A

World Bank – OP 8.00 – Rapid Response to Crises and Emergencies

Agency name	WB – OP 8.00
Type of mechanism/ instrument	Policy guidance and funding instrument for rapid response
Mechanism/ instrument objective	OP 8.00 objectives include: Rebuilding and restoring physical assets Restoring the means of production and economic activities Preserving or restoring essential services Establishing and/or preserving human, institutional, and/or social capital, including economic reintegration of vulnerable groups Facilitating peacebuilding Assisting with the crucial initial stages of building capacity for longer-term reconstruction, disaster management, and risk reduction Supporting measures to mitigate or avert the potential effects of imminent emergencies or future emergencies or crises in countries at high risk
Legal basis	N/A
Annual Budget	N/A - Regular IDA-IBRD funding, Post-Conflict Fund, LICUS Trust Fund, Global Fund for Disaster Reduction and Recovery
Geographical/ operational scope	Geographical scope: N/A Operational scope : N/A
Institutional set-up	Emergencies monitored by the Regional Vice President (RVP)/Managing Director (MD) of the affected Region with a notice to the Chief Financial Officer (CFO) and the Vice President, Operations Policy and Country Services. A Rapid Response Committee may be established
Deployment time frame	Average time frame: 10 weeks
Documented impacts	Between 1 March 2007 and 15 February 2008, 42 Emergency Recovery Operations have been approved, of which 17 were processed under the *Rapid Response to Crises and Emergencies* policy, worth over USD 800 million. Projects include urban and social rehabilitation in the Democratic Republic of the Congo, infrastructure rehabilitation in CAR, emergency post-conflict assistance in Cote d'Ivoire, three projects in Liberia including a community empowerment project, a health systems project and an infrastructure development project, an emergency social protection implementation grant for Lebanon, and an energy system delivery programme in Timor Leste

Non-governmental organisations

FEWER-Eurasia – Various Instruments/Mechanisms

Agency name	FEWER-Eurasia
Type of mechanism/ instrument	Peace Reconstruction Pool; Humanitarian Dialogue Roundtables; Constructive Direct Action (Mechanisms for development of common positions and dialogue)
Mechanism/ instrument objective	The promotion of a just and lasting peace in conflict-affected areas of the North Caucasus
Legal basis	N/A
Annual Budget	N/A
Geographical/ operational scope	Geographical scope: North Caucasus Operational scope: Violent conflict and human rights abuses
Institutional set-up	Mechanisms are managed by FEWER-Eurasia
Deployment time frame	Subject to funding availability – ranges between three months and one year
Documented impacts	Contributions to a decrease in number of disappearances in Chechnya

Foundation for Co-Existence – Program on Human Security and Co-Existence

Agency name	FCE-PHSC
Type of mechanism/ instrument	Direct preventive actions through Co-Existence Committees (CECs) and local/national level advocacy for response
Mechanism/ instrument objective	Prevention of violent conflict and incidents of violence at a local level
Legal basis	N/A
Annual Budget	USD 350 000 (approximately EUR 225 000) Main donors: The British High Commission in Sri Lanka , The Royal Norwegian Embassy in Sri Lanka, and the World Bank
Geographical/ operational scope	Geographical scope: Sri Lanka Operational scope: Violent conflict and inter-community violence
Institutional set-up	The PHSC is a programme of the Foundation for Co-Existence
Deployment time frame	24 hours to one week
Documented impacts	Various, including Eastern Province case (see Case Study 3 in Box 3.3in main report)

Foundation for Tolerance International – Non-Violent Conflict Resolution Programme

Agency name	FTI-NVCRP
Type of mechanism/ instrument	Direct preventive actions and local/national level advocacy for response
Mechanism/ instrument objective	Assist conflicting parties and decision makers in identifying and implementing nonviolent methods of conflict resolution
Legal basis	N/A
Annual Budget	EUR 64 000
Geographical/ operational scope	Geographical scope: Kyrgyzstan and border areas Operational scope : Violent conflict
Institutional set-up	The NVCRP is a programme of the Foundation for Tolerance International
Deployment time frame	2-3 days
Documented impacts	Two successful preventive interventions in Naryn oblast and one in Osh oblast (Uzgen rayon)

OECD PUBLISHING, 2, rue André-Pascal, 75775 PARIS CEDEX 16
PRINTED IN FRANCE
(43 2009 14 1 P) ISBN 978-92-64-05980-1 – No. 56681 2009